XML

in easy steps

MIKE MCGRATH

COMPUTER
STEP

In easy steps is an imprint of Computer Step
Southfield Road . Southam
Warwickshire CV47 0FB . England

http://www.ineasysteps.com

Notice of Liability
Every effort has been made to ensure that this book contains accurate and current information. However, Computer Step and the author shall not be liable for any loss or damage suffered by readers as a result of any information contained herein.

Trademarks
All trademarks are acknowledged as belonging to their respective companies.

Printed and bound in the United Kingdom

ISBN 1-84078-124-6

Table of Contents

XMLSchema simple types   49

4

XMLSchema complex types   67

5

XML namespaces   85

6

Introducing XML

Welcome to the exciting world of XML. This initial chapter looks at how the eXtensible Markup Language (XML) has evolved and a simple example demonstrates how it can be displayed in a web browser. The features and benefits of specialized XML editors are also discussed and illustrated.

Covers

Chapter One

XML in this book

This book is an introduction to the eXtensible Markup Language (XML) using examples to demonstrate each step. XML has been created to overcome some of the limitations that are found in the Hypertext Markup Language (HTML). Because HTML is so hugely popular many of its features have been incorporated into XML and will seem familiar if you know a little about HTML.

Microsoft's goal is 100% adherence to the XML standard. XML is core to their .net strategy.

The two main applications for XML are the publication of web pages and the exchange of information. This book focuses mostly upon publishing XML data on web pages in order to teach the beginner about XML syntax, schemas, links, transformation and styling. These are the areas you need to learn in order to start creating your own XML applications.

What you need to know

The ideas and examples given in this book will be more readily understood if you can already read and write basic HTML pages. It would also help to understand a couple of the later examples if you could read, and comprehend, a basic JavaScript. You do not need to be an expert coder, or a JavaScript guru.

Platforms and parsers

XML is a cross-platform technology but the Microsoft Internet Explorer web browser best supports XML features. Consequently all the featured examples relate to Internet Explorer on the Windows platform.

The code in a XML document must be processed by a small application called a 'parser'. There are several parsers available but this book uses only the Microsoft XML parser (MSXML). In order to process XML documents in Internet Explorer this must first be installed on your computer.

The MSXML parser can be freely downloaded from the web at **http://msdn.microsoft.com/downloads** and comprises a single file named **msxml4.msi** (4.7Mb). This file uses the Windows Installer version 2.0 to install the parser on your computer. Recent versions of the Windows operating system include the Windows Installer but this can be freely downloaded from Microsoft if required.

Markup language evolution

Historically, the desire to have text printed in specific formats meant that original manuscripts had to be 'marked up' with annotation to indicate to the book-printer how sections of text should be displayed.

This annotation had to be concise and needed to be understood both by the printer and the text originator.

A series of commonly recognised abbreviations therefore formed the basis of a markup 'language'.

HTML is a modern markup language that uses common abbreviations called 'tags' to advise a web browser how the author would like to have the web page displayed.

It was devised in the late 1980s by a British scientist named Tim Berners-Lee and improved in 1993 when a college student named Marc Anderssen added an image tag so that HTML could display images in addition to text.

The simplicity of HTML led it to become very popular and by the mid 1990s various web browsers that were fighting for market share began to add proprietary tags to effectively create their own versions of HTML.

W3C is the recognised body that oversees standards on the web. You can find the latest developments on their informative website at:

www.w3c.org

The World Wide Web Consortium (W3C) recognised the danger that HTML could become fragmented and acted to create a standard to which all web browsers should adhere.

The W3C standard was widely adopted but HTML remained simply a means to indicate how content should be displayed.

XML has been developed by the W3C to overcome this limitation and provide a better means to manage information that the growth of the Internet now demands.

Both HTML and XML are themselves based upon the Standard Generalized Markup Language (SGML) and so they share some common features.

XML is not intended as a replacement for HTML but the important development is that XML can describe content data in addition to indicating how it should be displayed.

What's wrong with HTML

The way that a web browser interprets a HTML document provides maximum tolerance for the correctness of the code in order to make HTML as user-friendly as possible.

For instance, consider the code in this HTML document:

```
<Center>
<p>The World's Most Popular web Browser <HR>
<Img src=ie_logo.gif >
```

This code has no <html>, <head> or <title> tags and the tags that are used have a mixture of uppercase and lowercase characters. The <center> and <p> tags have no matching </center> or </p> closing tags. Also the value of the 'src' attribute in the <img> tag is not enclosed in quotes.

All of these points illustrate strictly incorrect HTML code yet the document displays correctly in Internet Explorer:

It is estimated that over 50% of program code in a web browser is just there to provide tolerance for poor HTML coding.

The easy-going nature of HTML is also its downfall because the size of the web browser application is greatly enlarged with programming code that provides these tolerances.

An increasing variety of devices are being used to access web documents and these require a slim browser to process both content and data in a way that HTML does not provide.

The XML solution

Unlike PCs, devices such as Personal Digital Assistants (PDAs), Cellphones and Web-Pads cannot afford the luxury of a 10Mb web browser that is bloated with program code to tolerate poor HTML code and is, therefore, slower to use.

To overcome this problem XML adopts a very strict syntax so browsers do not need to include any tolerance code. This means that the browser can be made both smaller and faster.

XML code looks very much like HTML code, complete with tags, attributes and values.

Unlike HTML there are no predefined tags in XML.

But XML has no predefined tags and is not used to create web pages directly.

Instead XML allows you to create your own custom markup tags and define how these tags can be used.

The combination of tag and content in a defined document structure is where the power of XML lies.

Custom tags can also contain attributes to describe the content that is enclosed by the tag.

These data attributes can be used by external programs to extract information from a whole range of data by seeking out those tags with specific attribute values.

For instance, a custom <book> tag with an attribute called 'publisher' might be used to markup a range of book titles from a variety of publishers. Titles from one particular publisher could be extracted by seeking <book> tags which contain an appropriate value in their publisher attribute.

The custom tags are not limited to a single attribute and can contain several attributes to describe different aspects of the enclosed data.

Once created, XML tagged data can be reused whenever it is required to extract whatever information is sought.

The extracted data may be used in a variety of ways by the external application, including formatting into a web page.

Hello World

In keeping with tradition, here is a first simple XML document featuring the customary 'Hello World' message:

hello.xml

```
<?xml version="1.0" ?>

<root>

    <greeting> Hello World </greeting>

</root>
```

XML syntax is discussed in more detail in Chapter 2.

The first line of this XML document, and all others, is a declaration that informs the browser's XML parser to expect to process some XML code.

All XML documents must have a main tag element that encloses all other elements. The main element is more correctly called the 'root' element. In this example the root element is actually named 'root' although it could be called any other valid name.

A second tag element, called 'greeting', surrounds the string of characters that comprise the Hello World message.

Opening **hello.xml** in Internet Explorer may seem somewhat disappointing as it appears to merely display the source code:

The source code is displayed as a Tree View of the XML document. Click on the symbol before the opening <root> tag to collapse or expand the contained tags.

The output has, in fact, been checked as correctly forming a XML document and the text content is displayed bold. If the XML document is not well-formed, Internet Explorer will display an error message together with a helpful comment indicating the cause of the error.

Displaying XML content

A style sheet can be specified in the hello.xml document in order to make the Hello World message on the facing page display in Internet Explorer .

The style sheet can use familiar Cascading StyleSheets (CSS) rules to tell the browser how to display the contents of the custom <greeting> element in **hello.xml**.

hello.xml

```
<?xml version="1.0" ?>

<?xml:stylesheet href="hello.css" type="text/css" ?>

<root>
    <greeting>Hello World</greeting>
</root>
```

hello.css

```
greeting {
        font:bold italic 26pt;
        color: silver;
}
```

A second line has been added to the code for the **hello.xml** document that is listed on the facing page.

This new line instructs the browser's XML parser to look for a style sheet named hello.css in the same directory that contains **hello.xml**.

The hello.css style sheet instructs the browser to display the contents of the custom <greeting> element in a specified colour and font style.

This is just one way to use the tagged data in a XML file.

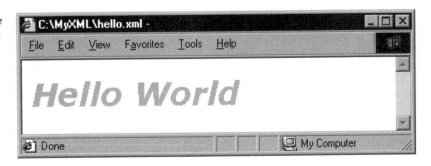

XML editors

XML documents are just plain text so they can be written in any simple text editor such as Windows Notepad.

However, there are several specialized XML editors available that offer significant benefits when creating a XML project.

Most XML editors have a text window where the XML code can be written and also a preview window that will instantly display how the output will display in a web browser.

So a specialized XML editor enables a XML project to be written, previewed and amended quickly.

Also a XML editor will normally offer coloured syntax highlighting of XML keywords to clarify the code.

Schema rules specify how XML tags may be used and are explained in full later in this book.

To ensure that your XML code is error-free a XML editor will have a syntax checker and a validator to check against schema rules that may apply to the code.

These and other labour-saving features make the creation of XML projects in a specialized XML editor preferable to using a standard text editor.

The most widely used XML editor is the XML Spy application that is available for download as a fully-featured 30-day evaluation at **http://www.xmlspy.com**.

To use XML Spy beyond this time limit will require you to obtain a registered copy.

XML Spy is a very comprehensive professional XML editor and this is reflected in its registration cost.

The XML Spy editor has been used to create all the examples featured in this book.

For a lower priced XML editor try the XMLwriter editor that is available as a 30-day trial from **http://xmlwriter.net**.

The following few pages illustrate the XML Spy interface and demonstrate some of the features mentioned above together with other useful features that are included.

XML Spy editor views

XML Spy offers two different views of the editor window where XML code can be created or edited.

The normal text view is selected using the Text View ⊞ button on the toolbar so that the **hello.xml** document appears in the XML Spy editor window like this :

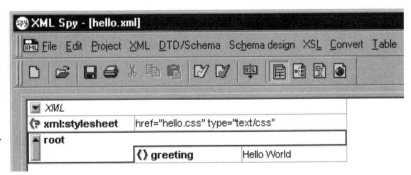

Alternatively a Grid View of the XML document can be displayed using the Grid View ⊞ button on the toolbar to change the appearance of the **hello.xml** document to this:

*To make Text View the default click Tools > Options and select the File Types tab. Now choose the **.xml** file type from the list then select the Text View radio button in the Default View panel. Finally push the Apply button to set the view.*

Experienced XML coders will find the Grid View useful but beginners should start out writing code with the Text View.

This can be made the default view so that XML documents will always be displayed in XML Spy using the Text View.

XML Spy browser view

XML Spy can quickly provide a preview of how a document in the editor window will appear in a web browser by clicking the Browser View button on the toolbar.

The XML document will be checked to ensure that it is well-formed then it will be displayed as a Tree in the Browser View if no style sheet has been specified:

It is better to have the Browser View always open in a new window. Click Tools > Options and select the View tab, then check the checkbox in the Browser View panel and click the Apply button.

In the event that the XML document does specify a style sheet the Browser View will apply the style rules and display the final output:

XSD Schema Documents and XSL Style Sheets are explained in detail later in this book.

Other buttons on the toolbar include the Schema Design View button, that can be used to display a XSD Schema Document in a special Grid View, and the XSL Transformation button, that is used to transform XML data into a HTML document using a XSL style sheet.

XML Spy code validation

The ability to check that XML code is well-formed and validate it against a set of schema rules is one of the most important facilities that XML Spy provides.

Clicking on the yellow Check Well-formedness button on the toolbar will test the XML document structure. If any errors are found they are reported with a helpful indication of their nature and location. Otherwise XML Spy confirms that the XML document is indeed well-formed.

DTD and XSD Schemas are explained in detail later in this book.

Clicking on the green Validate button will test the document structure and also validate it against rules in any specified DTD or XSD Schema. If errors exist they are reported with a helpful indication of their nature, otherwise XML Spy pronounces the XML document to be valid.

An additional line of code has been added into the **hello.xml** document shown in the illustration below. This points to the location of a schema file named **hello.dtd** containing rules governing the <root> and <greeting> tags. XML Spy has validated that the tags are used appropriately and so confirms that the XML document is valid.

Notice that when schemas are specified, the main XML declaration should include an attribute denoting that this is not a standalone document.

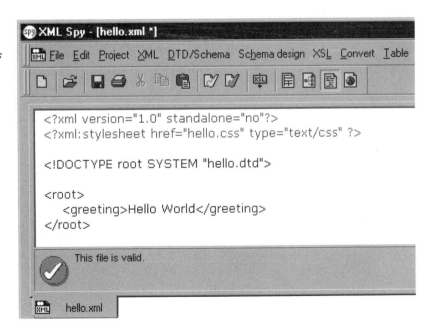

Microsoft XML Notepad

For experienced XML coders Microsoft produce a simple yet effective XML editor that is based upon the Tree View of a XML document.

This allows the quick creation of a basic XML document without the need to type opening and closing tags around the actual content data.

The Notepad window is split into two panes. The left pane shows the document tree structure illustrating each tag element and offsets those elements that are nested within other elements. The right pane lists the corresponding value of each individual element.

Right-click on any element shown in the left pane to open a context menu that allows new elements to be added or existing elements to be amended, duplicated or deleted.

XML Notepad is a free product that is available for download from Microsoft at www.microsoft.com – search for "XML Notepad".

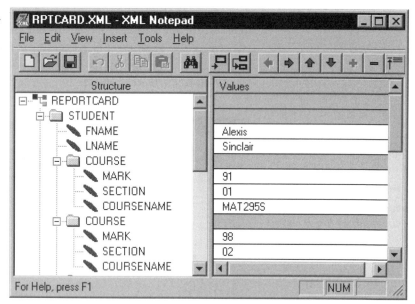

XML Notepad is well worth trying when you are comfortable with the essentials of XML. The format that it uses is a useful stopping-off point between the Text View and the Tree View in the XML Spy editor.

XML basics

This chapter introduces the basic requirements of XML code. It illustrates by example how to create a XML document with correctly formed syntax and demonstrates how a complete XML document can be formatted for display in a web browser with a style sheet.

Covers

Chapter Two

What is XML?

Like most good ideas, XML is basically a very simple idea that can be put to good use in many situations. It is not intended to be a direct replacement for the general-purpose markup that is provided by HTML describing how content should be displayed. Instead XML offers a means to define and construct other custom markup languages with tags you name yourself and rules which you define for how those tags can be used. So because XML is a language that describes other languages it is termed as being a 'meta-language'.

The two words that should be most strongly associated with any definition of XML are 'structure' and 'data'.

Custom markup languages constructed in XML will arrange data in a structured manner so it can be accessed and manipulated in a variety of ways. For instance, you could use XML to create a custom markup language called 'EruptML' to describe the data on all active volcanoes.

Technically the custom markup languages that are created in XML are known as 'XML applications' but, to avoid confusion with normal software applications, that term is not used in this book.

The mechanics of making up your own markup tags are covered in this chapter of the book together with an explanation of the syntax rules that must be obeyed to ensure that your XML document has well-formed code.

Following after this basic grounding are chapters explaining how to define rules for your tags with a Document Type Definition (DTD) or with the more comprehensive XMLSchema language.

Finally, after learning how to create a well-formed XML document with custom tags that are valid to your defined rules, we can look at how the structured data in the document can actually be used.

Using data in a XML document often employs other XML technologies which are explored in the later chapters in the book.

But first, discover the basics of XML in this chapter...

Tag format

XML element tags look much like those you see in HTML but, unlike HTML, there are no pre-defined elements. Greater care must be taken with XML elements to ensure that they adhere to strict syntax rules to make the XML document well-formed.

Case

XML is a case-sensitive language, so for instance the tags <address>, <Address> and <ADDRESS> are considered to be three separate unrelated elements in XML. It is recommended that you use only lowercase for element names to avoid confusion.

Naming conventions

Omission of closing tags is an error that prevents the XML document being well-formed.

Element names in XML may only start with either a letter or underscore character. The rest of the name may consist of any mixture of letter, number, underscore, dot or hyphen characters. Spaces are not allowed in element names nor can the name begin with the string 'xml' which is reserved for the XML specification. <mytag>, <_mytag> and <my-tag1.extra> are all valid names. <1mytag>, <my tag> and <xml-tag> are all invalid names.

Closing tags

Every XML element must have an associated closing tag to be valid. Empty elements that contain no data can use a closing tag or the shorthand method that puts a '/' at the end of the opening tag. Regular and empty XML elements might look like this:

```
<mytag> data </mytag>
<emptytag/>
```

Empty tags are usually only included in a document for the value of an attribute that they contain.

Attributes

Either single or double quotes can be used for attribute values but double quotes are recommended.

XML elements can contain one or more attributes which define values that are relevant to that element. Each attribute has a name, following the same naming conventions as the element name, and a value assigned with the '=' operator. Unlike HTML, all attribute values must be enclosed in quotation marks to be valid.

```
<security level= "classified"> Confidential </security>
```

The XML declaration

The start of the very first line of every XML document should contain the XML declaration. This identifies the document to be a XML document and defines the version of XML being used.

The XML declaration is stated in a special tag that starts '<?' and ends '?>' to denote that it contains a processing instruction. This type of tag can also be used to state other processing instructions, such as specifying the style sheet that is to be used with that XML document.

Inside the tag, the element is named 'xml' to denote that it is part of the XML specification itself. To define the XML version being used, the tag adds an attribute named 'version' that is assigned the version number as its value. Currently the version is 1.0 so the XML declaration looks like this:

```
<?xml version="1.0"?>
```

All attribute values must be enclosed by quotation marks.

The XML declaration can also contain additional attributes to define other information about the document such as character encoding or document dependency.

Character encoding in XML follows the Unicode standard which means that the XML processor will recognize UTF-8 encoded documents, such as those written in English, and also UTF-16 encoded documents, such as those written in Japanese. Most XML processors also support the Latin-1 encoding (ISO-8859-1), that is used by Windows, but encodings other than UTF-8 or UTF-16 can be specified in the XML declaration like this example:

```
<?xml version="1.0" encoding="ISO-8859-1"?>
```

The XML declaration may include an attribute called 'standalone' to specify if that document uses other documents. This attribute can only have a value of either 'yes' or 'no'. Most XML documents use other files, such as a style sheet and schema, but completely independent XML documents might start with this declaration:

```
<?xml version="1.0" standalone="yes"?>
```

Elements

Every valid XML document must always have one single element that entirely encloses all the other elements in the document. This element is called the 'root' element.

Elements that are directly contained within the root element are said to be 'nested' within the root element. Further elements can be nested within those elements to form a sort of hierarchy.

An element that is enclosed by another element is called a 'child' of the containing element. Conversely the containing element is called the 'parent' of the enclosed element.

In the code shown below the root element is named 'personnel'. The personnel root element contains two child elements that are each named 'entry'. Each entry element encloses its own child element called 'name' that contains some content data.

 If the elements are not correctly nested the XML document will not be well-formed.

```xml
<?xml version="1.0" ?>
<personnel>
   <entry>
      <name>John Smith</name>
   </entry>
   <entry>
      <name>Sally Jones</name>
   </entry>
</personnel>
```

It is important to note that all elements must be correctly nested by writing their closing inner tags before writing the closing tag for their outer parent element.

The hierarchical nature of the elements in a XML document can be seen as a tree of elements, with the root element as its base.

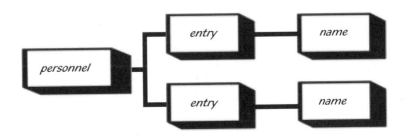

Element attributes

One, or more, attributes can be added to an element to store additional information about the element's actual content. This information about other data is called 'meta-information'.

Each attribute must have a name and a value.

The attribute value is assigned to the attribute name using the '=' operator and the value must be enclosed in quotes. If the assigned value itself contains a quoted string the type of quotation marks must differ from those used to enclose the entire value. For instance, if double quotes are used to enclose the whole value then use single quotes for the string like this:

```
<name familiar="'Jack'">John Smith</name>
```

When naming attributes, you must follow the same naming conventions that are used when naming elements – see page 21.

The attributes in an element must each have a unique name to avoid confusing the XML parser. Also the value of an attribute cannot contain a '<' character, but this can be represented with the entity reference '<' instead.

An alternative way to attach meta-information to element data is to use nested elements. The attribute example shown above is included in the code below using this alternative method:

```
<?xml version="1.0" ?>
<personnel>
  <entry>
    <name>John Smith</name>
    <familiar>'Jack'</familiar>
  </entry>
  <entry>
    <name>Sally Jones</name>
    <tel>555-1234</tel>
    <tel preferred="true">555-8282</tel>
  </entry>
</personnel>
```

Attributes are generally less suited to containing explicit data but more typically are useful to supply information about the status or preference of an element's actual content. The code above illustrates this when stating a preferred contact telephone number.

Empty elements

Elements that do not enclose any child elements or textual data are called 'empty elements'. Although they have no content that can be written out as text, empty elements are useful to include information inside their attributes. For instance, you might want to include information regarding the source of an image file that is relevant to a particular entry.

Empty elements can have a normal closing tag, or can use the shorthand method that combines both tags by adding a closing slash at the end of the opening tag.

The code below demonstrates both methods being used to indicate the source of relevant image files in the element called 'photo':

Attribute values must always be enclosed in quotes.

```
<?xml version="1.0" ?>
<personnel>
   <entry>
      <name>John Smith</name>
      <familiar>'Jack'</familiar>
      <photo filename="jsmith.jpg"></photo>
      <tel>555-6363</tel>
   </entry>
   <entry>
      <name>Sally Jones</name>
      <familiar>'Sal'</familiar>
      <photo filename="sjones.jpg" />
      <tel>555-1234</tel>
      <tel preferred="true">555-8282</tel>
   </entry>
</personnel>
```

It does not matter whether empty elements are closed with the shorthand method or with a separate closing tag as XML regards both methods as equally correct.

Empty elements, or any other elements, that are not closed will mean that the XML document is not well-formed and will cause an error to be generated by the XML parser.

Comments

It is always good practice to add comments to any source code to annotate sections of the code so that their purpose is clear when read by a third party, or when the source code is revisited after a period of time.

XML uses exactly the same syntax as HTML for comments so that any text that is inserted between '<!--' and '-->' will be ignored by the XML parser.

A double hyphen may not be used inside comment tags as this will confuse the parser. This means that a comment may not be nested inside another comment. Also note that comments should not be added inside an element tag but must appear either before or after a complete tag.

It is sometimes useful to temporarily add comment tags around a section of XML code to hide it from the parser during development or debugging. This is called 'commenting-out' and can be used to isolate a piece of code that is creating an error so that it can be identified and rectified.

The comment text may be just a few words or many lines but the entire comment will be invisible to both the XML parser and the web browser. The example below includes several comments:

Add a date comment to each XML document to establish when the code was created or when it was last updated.

```
<?xml version="1.0" ?>
<!-- staff list, last updated 5th April 2003 -->
<personnel>
<!-- staff member -->
  <entry>
    <!-- full name -->
    <name>John Smith</name>
     <!-- commonly known as -->
    <familiar>'Jack'</familiar>
    <!-- mugshot -->
    <photo filename="jsmith.jpg"></photo>
    <!-- home telephone number -->
    <tel>555-6363</tel>
  </entry>
</personnel>
```

Character entities

The XML specification predefines five special pieces of code for characters that are normally recognised as part of the XML language itself. These are called 'character entities' and they must be used if you want to include those characters as part of an element's content. Character entities use a special syntax to represent the character in a way that avoids the XML parser interpreting the character as code.

The standard XML character entities are as follows:

- < represents the '<' left angle bracket.

- > represents the '>' right angle bracket.

- & represents the '&' ampersand character.

- ' represents the "' single quote apostrophe.

- " represents the "" double quotation mark.

XML also supports character references that create a character using its Unicode character code. These are written in the XML document as '&#nnn;' where 'nnn' is the reference number. This is useful to add characters that are not available on your keyboard.

The Windows Character Map application can be used to find the Unicode reference number of many characters.

```xml
<?xml version="1.0"?>
<root>
  <drill>Black &amp; Decker</drill>
  <lager>Gr&#252;nhalle</lager>
</root>
```

```
C:\MyXML\entity.xml                                    _ □ ×
  File   Edit   View   Favorites   Tools   Help

    <?xml version="1.0" ?>
  - <root>
      <drill>Black & Decker</drill>
      <lager>Grünhalle</lager>
    </root>

  Done                                      My Computer
```

CDATA blocks

Character data that is not required to be interpreted by the XML parser can be 'escaped' inside a CDATA block of code in a XML document.

The CDATA blocks are enclosed by '<![CDATA]' and ']]>' so that anything between will be preserved literally in the document. This is useful to incorporate examples of markup without having to escape all the recognised markup characters individually.

In the code below a CDATA block includes an entire XML document that is preserved when viewed in Internet Explorer:

A XML document can have multiple CDATA blocks but they cannot be nested inside each other.

```
<?xml version="1.0"?>
<root>
  <title>CDATA Example</title>
  <![CDATA[
    <?xml version="1.0">
    <root>
     <greeting>Hello World</greeting>
    </root>
  ]]>

</root>
```

```
C:\MyXML\cdata.xml - Microsoft Internet Explorer

File  Edit  View  Favorites  Tools  Help

  <?xml version="1.0" ?>
- <root>
    <title>CDATA Example</title>
- <![CDATA[

      <?xml version="1.0">
      <root>
        <greeting>Hello World</greeting>
      </root>

  ]]>
  </root>

Done                                        My Computer
```

XML example document

The XML basics that are demonstrated in this chapter are evidence that XML is itself very simple. The power of XML lies in what can be achieved with the data that is described in XML.

To summarise XML syntax, the code below incorporates some of the features of XML in a single document:

personnel.xml

The XML parser ignores indents and line breaks so XML code is normally formatted to make it more easily human-readable.

```
<?xml version="1.0" standalone="no"?>

<?xml:stylesheet href="personnel.css" type="text/css" ?>

<!-- management list, last updated 5th April 2003 -->

<personnel>

  <heading>Company Managers</heading>

  <entry>
     <job>Sales &amp; Marketing Manager</job>
     <name>John Smith</name>
     <tel preferred="true">555-9494</tel>
     <tel>555-6363</tel>
  </entry>

  <entry>
     <job>Accounts Manager</job>
     <name>Sally Jones</name>
     <tel>555-8282</tel>
     <photo filename="sjones.jpg" />
  </entry>

  <entry>
     <job>Production Manager</job>
     <name>Bob Solomon</name>
     <tel>555-7171</tel>
  </entry>

</personnel>
```

The style sheet referred to in this document is shown overleaf, together with an illustration of how this XML data may be displayed by the style sheet in a web browser.

Example document output

The style sheet shown below defines the style rules for the elements in the XML document detailed on the previous page. These can be used to display the XML data in a web browser.

personnel.css

```
heading {
    font-family:cursive;
    display:block;
    font:bold 18pt;
}

job {
    display:block;
    font-weight:bold;
    background:gray; color:white;
    padding:2px;
    margin-top:10px; }

name { font-style:italic }

tel { display:block; font-weight:bold }
```

Document Type Definition

This chapter shows how to define rules for the elements of a XML document using a Document Type Definition (DTD). Examples demonstrate how an element can be controlled.

Covers

Chapter Three

Introducing schemas

In order to control the way that elements can be used inside a XML document a set of rules can be written governing its elements and their attributes.

This set of rules is called a 'schema'.

Although a XML document does not strictly need to have a schema its inclusion does bring several benefits:

- The XML parser carries out validation to ensure that the XML document structure follows the defined schema rules.

- A schema can declare default values for element attributes.

- A single schema can be used by several XML documents to ensure their consistency.

If the elements in a XML document are not used in accordance with its schema rules the XML parser will declare that document to be invalid.

'Well-formed' documents have correct XML syntax whereas a 'valid' document also agrees with defined schema rules.

The schema must be sure to define a rule for each element and every attribute that appears in the XML document in order for it to be declared valid by the XML parser.

A schema may be written either as a Document Type Definition (DTD), which is the method demonstrated in this chapter, or with the more comprehensive XMLSchema language that is covered in the following two chapters of this book.

A DTD that will only be used by a single XML document can be written internally within that document. More commonly the DTD will be created as a separate file with a **.dtd** file extension.

XML documents that are to be validated against an external DTD specify its location to the XML parser by quoting its URL in a DTD declaration within the XML document.

The DTD declaration

To declare a DTD to be used by a XML document you must add a <!DOCTYPE> statement to the XML document. This first states the name of the root element of that XML document followed by the schema rules to be applied.

The declaration for an internal DTD might look like this:

Notice the square brackets in this example that must surround the schema in any internal DTD.

```
<?xml version="1.0"?>

<!DOCTYPE fruit [

   (schema rules are added here)

] >

<fruit>
   <apple>Golden delicious</apple>
</fruit>
```

To change this example to an external DTD would require the schema rules to be written in a separate file that the DTD declaration can point to as a URL.

For DTDs that have been created solely for your own purposes the <!DOCTYPE> statement should precede the URL by the keyword SYSTEM to denote that it is not for widespread use.

Also remember to include the 'standalone' attribute in the XML declaration with its value set to 'no' because a XML document using an external DTD is not a standalone document.

So now the external DTD declaration might look like this:

```
<?xml version="1.0" standalone="no"?>

<!DOCTYPE fruit SYSTEM
               "http://domain/xml/fruit.dtd" >

<fruit>
   <apple>Golden delicious</apple>
</fruit>
```

Declaring public DTDs

For DTDs that are intended for widespread use the <!DOCTYPE> statement should precede the URL by the keyword 'PUBLIC', to denote that it is for general public use.

Also the DTD should be named using a standard naming format to create a 'Formal Public Identifier' (FPI), like this example:

-//MikeMcGrath//DTD FruitVarieties//EN//

standard   *owner*   *descriptive label*   *language*

A DTD name using the FPI format can start with a '+' if the DTD has been approved by a recognised standards body, like the ISO. Otherwise it should start with a '-' like the example above.

After the '//' delimiter the DTD name states the name of its owner. This will be the person or organization that wrote and maintains the DTD.

The next part of the DTD name contains the term 'DTD', followed by a space, then a chosen descriptive label 'FruitVarieties'.

A full list of the ISO two-letter language abbreviations can be found on-line at (no spaces):

http://www.unicode.org/ unicode/onlinedat/ languages.html

Finally the DTD name states the language that is used in the DTD by specifying the ISO standard two-letter abbreviation. The example above specifies that English language is used by stating the ISO standard abbreviation of 'EN'.

The DTD name can be used by the XML parser to locate the latest version of the DTD on the Internet. If the DTD cannot be found using its name then the specified URL address is used instead.

A typical external public DTD declaration might look like this:

```
<?xml version="1.0" standalone="no"?>

<!DOCTYPE fruit PUBLIC
        "-//MikeMcGrath//DTD FruitVarieties//EN//"
        "http://domain/xml/fruit.dtd" >

<fruit>
   <apple>Golden delicious</apple>
</fruit>
```

Defining elements

The schema rules for each element in a XML document are defined using an <!ELEMENT> declaration in the DTD. These rules specify which elements can be nested within other elements, and the allowable content for each element.

There must be precisely one <!ELEMENT> declaration for each element and they must contain the element name exactly as it appears in the XML document. An element type declaration can specify allowable content from the following table:

EMPTY	An empty element, such as <image />
ANY	Element will accept any content
(#PCDATA)	Text content that is not part of markup
(Child element)	Element that may be nested

PCDATA stands for 'Parsed Character Data' and an element that is defined to contain '#PCDATA' will contain text content.

Note that #PCDATA and any specified child elements must be surrounded by parentheses in the <!ELEMENT> declaration. The allowable content type appears after a space following the element name. The internal DTD example below specifies that the <fruit> root element must contain an <apple> child element which, in turn, can contain only text content:

fruit.xml

```
<?xml version="1.0" ?>

<!DOCTYPE fruit [

  <!ELEMENT fruit (apple)>

  <!ELEMENT apple (#PCDATA)>

]>

<fruit>
  <apple>Golden delicious</apple>
</fruit>
```

Sequential child elements

An <!ELEMENT> type declaration in a DTD may specify multiple child elements that are to be nested inside that parent element.

The name of each child element to be nested is specified in a comma-delimited list, in the same sequential order that the elements should appear in the XML document.

The entire list is contained within parentheses in the <!ELEMENT> type declaration of the parent element.

This DTD defines a sequence of child elements that should each appear once in the parent root element of the XML document:

The elements that are defined in a sequence could each contain further nested elements.

```
<?xml version="1.0" ?>

<!DOCTYPE fruit[
   <!ELEMENT fruit (apple,orange,pear)>
   <!ELEMENT apple (#PCDATA)>
   <!ELEMENT orange (#PCDATA)>
   <!ELEMENT pear (#PCDATA)>
]>

<fruit>
   <apple>Golden delicious</apple>
   <orange>Seville</orange>
   <pear>Conference</pear>
</fruit>
```

```
C:\MyXML\fruit.xml

File   Edit   View   Favorites   Tools   Help

   <?xml version="1.0" ?>
   <!DOCTYPE fruit (View Source for full doctype...)>
 - <fruit>
      <apple>Golden delicious</apple>
      <orange>Seville</orange>
      <pear>Conference</pear>
   </fruit>

Done                                          My Computer
```

Alternative child elements

An element may sometimes be required to contain a choice of content so allowable alternatives may be specified in its <!ELEMENT> type declaration.

The alternatives are separated by the '|' pipe symbol which is often used in programming languages, as it is here, to represent the boolean OR where choices can be made. Available alternatives can be just a single child element, or a sequence of child elements contained in their own parentheses, or even another pair of alternatives contained in their own parentheses.

Finally the entire statement of allowable alternatives should be enclosed in parentheses within the <!ELEMENT> type declaration.

In the DTD below the root parent <fruit> element may contain a single <apple> element. Alternatively it may contain an <orange> element then a <pear> element, in that order.

fruit_choice.dtd

```
<!ELEMENT fruit (apple | (orange, pear) )>
<!ELEMENT apple (#PCDATA)>
<!ELEMENT orange (#PCDATA)>
<!ELEMENT pear (#PCDATA)>
```

The two XML documents shown below use this DTD and are both declared to be valid by the XML parser:

fruits1.xml

```
<?xml version="1.0" ?>
<!DOCTYPE fruit SYSTEM "fruit_choice.dtd">

<fruit>
  <apple>Golden delicious</apple>
</fruit>
```

fruits2.xml

```
<?xml version="1.0" ?>
<!DOCTYPE fruit SYSTEM "fruit_choice.dtd">

<fruit>
  <orange>Seville</orange>
  <pear>Conference</pear>
</fruit>
```

Occurrence indicators

Child elements that are specified in an <!ELEMENT> declaration must normally appear exactly once in the parent element. The number of allowable occurrences can be changed, however, by adding special occurrence indicator symbols after a specified child element in the <!ELEMENT> type declaration.

The three possible occurrence indicators that may be used are listed in the following table together with a description of how they affect the rule for an element:

Adding occurrence indicators greatly enhances the flexibility of the <!ELEMENT> type declaration by allowing child elements to be optional or to be repeated within the parent element.

+	Allows the element to appear one or more times within the parent element. The element must be included and it can repeat indefinitely
*	Allows the element to appear zero or more times within the parent element. The element is optional but if it is included it can repeat indefinitely
?	Allows the element to appear zero or just once within the parent element. The element is optional but if it is included it cannot repeat

The following <!ELEMENT> declaration specifies child elements that can be nested in a parent element called <student>. The declaration allows one or more <name> child elements, optionally zero or more <tel> child elements, and optionally just one <address> child element:

```
<!ELEMENT student (name+,tel*,address?) >
```

Any of the occurrence indicators can be applied to a single element, a parenthesized sequence or a parenthesized choice. For instance, the following <!ELEMENT> declaration optionally allows zero or more occurrences of the <height>, <width>, <depth> sequence of child elements in a parent element called <box>:

```
<!ELEMENT box (height,width,depth)* ) >
```

Mixed content

The asterisk occurrence indicator can be used in an <!ELEMENT> type declaration to allow a parent element to contain mixed content of both PCDATA and child elements.

The list of allowable contents must have #PCDATA as its first item with the child elements following and each item in the list must be separated from the next by a '|' pipe symbol . The entire list should be enclosed in parentheses with the occurrence indicator asterisk following outside the final bracket.

In the following example mixed content is allowed in the parent <student> element which can contain text and optionally one or more occurrences of the <name>, <tel> and <id> child elements.

This method of allowing mixed content loses some control over the child elements because you cannot add individual occurrence indicators .

```xml
<?xml version="1.0" encoding="UTF-8"?>

<!DOCTYPE student [

   <!ELEMENT student (#PCDATA | name | tel | id)*>

   <!ELEMENT name (#PCDATA)>

   <!ELEMENT tel (#PCDATA)>

   <!ELEMENT id (#PCDATA)>
]>

<student>

   You can put text anywhere.

   <name>Andrew McGrath</name>
   <id>901356</id>

   You can put the elements in any order in the document.

   <name>David McGrath</name>
   <id>702457</id>

   You don't have to include all the elements.

</student>
```

Defining element attributes

Elements can be allowed to contain attributes that can store additional information regarding the element's content. An attribute must be defined in an '<!ATTLIST>' declaration within the DTD before it is allowed to be used in the element.

The <!ATTLIST> declaration first states the name of the element that will contain the attribute, then the name of the attribute itself.

Next the <!ATTLIST> declaration specifies that the attribute value will comprise character data by stating the keyword 'CDATA'. Alternatively a choice of content can be given if separated by a '|' pipe symbol and enclosed in parentheses.

Finally the <!ATTLIST> declaration can include a default value that must be contained in quotes. This will be the value assigned to the attribute unless another is explicitly set. The default value can be fixed to always remain assigned to the attribute by preceding the stated default value with the keyword '#FIXED'.

If no default value is supplied the declaration can include the '#REQUIRED' keyword to specify that the attribute must appear in the element and have a value assigned to it. Alternatively the '#IMPLIED' keyword can be used instead to allow the attribute to be optionally omitted from the element.

Always define each attribute in a separate <!ATTLIST> declaration to avoid confusion.

The example below declares an attribute called 'name' for an element called <student>. Its value may be character data, and the attribute is always required to be included in the element:

```
<!ATTLIST student name CDATA #REQUIRED>
```

This next example declares an attribute called 'gender' for the element called <student>. Its value may only be 'male' or 'female' and the attribute may be omitted from the element entirely:

```
<!ATTLIST student gender (male | female) #IMPLIED>
```

An element may have multiple attributes, but each one must be defined in the DTD. Each of these attributes can be defined consecutively in a single <!ATTLIST> declaration or they can be defined separately in individual <!ATTLIST> declarations.

The DTD declarations shown below specify that an element called <class> has an attribute called 'year' with a default value of '2002':

```
<!ELEMENT class (#PCDATA)>
<!ATTLIST class year CDATA "2002">
```

The <class> element can include the 'year' attribute with any value assigned to it. Importantly, if the attribute is omitted from the element tag in the XML document, the attribute, and its default value, is still recognised as being present by the XML parser.

All three of the following XML tags are valid for this class element:

```
<class year="2002">Web Design</class>
```

```
<class year="2005">Web Design</class>
```

```
<class>Web Design</class>
```

The #FIXED keyword could be added to the <!ATTLIST> declaration to ensure that the year attribute value could only be that specified by the default:

```
<!ATTLIST class year CDATA #FIXED "2002">
```

Details of using JavaScript with XML are given in Chapter 11.

Now the second XML tag shown above would be invalid.

With either the first or third tags included in the XML document the <class> element contains the 'year' attribute with the value of '2002' – viz. this example that uses JavaScript to explore the values in the XML document then write them out on a HTML page:

```
Tag Name: class
Tag Content: Web Design
Tag Attribute Name: year
Tag Attribute Value: 2002
```

Attribute value restrictions

DTDs do not provide a way to specify which data types may be used as attribute values, but there are some restrictions that can be applied using special keywords in the <!ATTLIST> declaration.

The 'NMTOKEN' keyword ensures that the attribute can only contain a value that is a single item without any whitespace. Also the value may only begin with a letter, digit, period, hyphen, colon or underscore character:

```
<?xml version="1.0"?>
<!DOCTYPE student[
  <!ELEMENT student (#PCDATA)>
  <!ATTLIST student number NMTOKEN #REQUIRED>
]>
<student number="12345">John Smith</student>
```

To allow the attribute value to contain a list of NMTOKEN items, that are each separated by whitespace, the plural version 'NMTOKENS' keyword can be used.

An ID attribute may not be #FIXED but may only be #IMPLIED or #REQUIRED.

Perhaps more usefully, the 'ID' keyword ensures that whatever value is assigned to the attribute is unique throughout that XML document. This is ideal for attributes that contain information such as unique product codes which are not to be repeated.

An ID attribute can only begin with a letter, colon or underscore. This means it may not contain purely numerical values unless they are prefixed with one of these valid beginning characters:

```
<?xml version="1.0"?>
<!DOCTYPE range[
    <!ELEMENT range (product)+ >
    <!ELEMENT product (#PCDATA)>
    <!ATTLIST product code ID #REQUIRED>
]>

<range>
  <product code="S123">Stanley screwdriver</product>
  <product code="B765">Bosch electric drill</product>
</range>
```

Referencing unique attributes

An attribute can be allowed to contain a value that refers to a unique ID attribute by specifying the 'IDREF' keyword in its <!ATTLIST> declaration.

This is useful to cross-reference elements against the unique attribute so that their association is made clear. For instance, the XML document below adds IDREF attributes to the <price> tags in order to clarify which product each price refers to:

Several IDREF attributes can refer to the same ID attribute – only the ID attribute needs to be unique in a XML document.

```
<?xml version="1.0" standalone="yes"?>
<!DOCTYPE range[
  <!ELEMENT range (product, price)+ >

  <!ELEMENT product (#PCDATA)>
  <!ATTLIST product code ID #REQUIRED>

  <!ELEMENT price (#PCDATA)>
  <!ATTLIST price code-ref IDREF #IMPLIED>
]>

<range>

  <product code="S123">Stanley screwdriver</product>
  <price code-ref="S123">£7.99</price>

  <product code="B765">Bosch electric drill</product>
  <price code-ref="B765">£39.50</price>

</range>
```

To allow an attribute value to contain a list of IDREF items, that are each separated by whitespace, the plural version 'IDREFS' keyword can be used. This could be useful in the above example to allow the <range> root element to have an attribute containing a list of all product codes by adding the following <!ATTLIST> declaration to the DTD:

```
<!ATTLIST range code-list IDREFS #IMPLIED>
```

So now the opening root element tag could look like this:

```
<range code-list="S123 B765">
```

General entities

A DTD allows you to define your own entity references. These can subsequently be used anywhere in the XML document, in both text and markup. This provides a handy way of creating shorthand abbreviations for strings of text that may be used frequently.

The general entity is first defined in an '<!ENTITY>' declaration in the DTD. This declaration includes a name for the entity followed by the complete string enclosed in quotation marks.

Referencing entities requires the same syntax used by the five predefined character entities demonstrated on page 27.

Once declared, the entity can be included in the XML document by using its name preceded by an ampersand and followed by a semi-colon. For instance, '&myname;' would refer to a general entity that had been named 'myname'. When a XML document is parsed by the browser any general entity references are automatically replaced by the string values which they represent.

General entities are also often used to create shorthand for character references like the example below that uses '©' to represent the '©' symbol:

```
<?xml version="1.0" encoding="UTF-8"?>

<!DOCTYPE root [

<!ELEMENT root (#PCDATA) >

<!ENTITY copy "&#169;">

<!ENTITY author "Mike McGrath">
]>

<root>Document &copy; &author; </root>
```

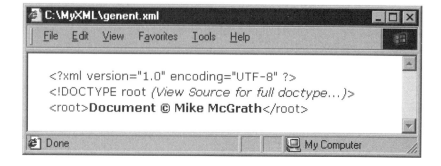

Parameter entities

Parameter entities, unlike general entities, can only appear within the DTD and must contain valid XML markup code. A parameter <!ENTITY> declaration first includes a percent symbol to denote that it is declaring a parameter entity rather than a general entity. Once declared the entity can be referenced using its name preceded by a '%' and followed by a semi-colon.

Parameter entities are often used to insert the contents of another file into a DTD. For example, a file containing a list of general entities that represent country names could be added into a DTD using a parameter entity. Each country name can then appear in the XML document using the appropriate general entity from the inserted list. This is far simpler than redefining the whole list.

The following code illustrates this example in action. Notice that the internal DTD contains an <!ENTITY> declaration, to define the parameter entity, then uses a reference to that parameter entity to make the list of general entities available from the external file:

europe.dtd

```
<!ENTITY at "Austria">
<!ENTITY be "Belgium">
<!ENTITY dk "Denmark">
<!ENTITY fi "Finland">
<!ENTITY fr "France">
<!ENTITY de "Germany">
<!-- and so on... -->
```

address.xml

```
<?xml version="1.0" encoding="UTF-8"?>
<!DOCTYPE address [
  <!ELEMENT address (city)*>
  <!ELEMENT city (#PCDATA)>
  <!ATTLIST city country CDATA #IMPLIED>

  <!ENTITY % europe SYSTEM "europe.dtd">

  %europe;
]>

<address>
  <city country="&fr;">Paris</city>
</address>
```

Unparsed entities

An entity that contains text or markup is usually read by the XML parser so it is known as 'a parsed' entity. Other types of content can be embedded into a XML file, however, using an 'unparsed' entity. As its name suggests, the content of this type of entity is not processed by the XML parser. An unparsed entity can contain virtually any sort of content including plain text, an image file, a sound file, a movie file or a PDF document.

An <!ENTITY> declaration for an unparsed entity specifies an entity name, as usual, then states a URL pointing to the content's location. This is followed by the keyword 'NDATA', to denote that this entity will contain unparsed data. Finally, the declaration states the name of a notation that will describe the unparsed data.

A '<!NOTATION>' declaration is used along with an unparsed entity to describe the data it contains. The description will typically be a MIME type like 'image/jpeg', but could also be a URL giving the location of an application that could handle the data content, or any other indicator of how the content could be handled. The <!NOTATION> declaration first states its name, then gives the data description as a MIME type or URL.

The following DTD creates unparsed entities for a variety of different content and the entity notations describe each one by their MIME types:

ndata.dtd

```
<!ENTITY mypic SYSTEM "mypic.gif" NDATA gif>
<!NOTATION gif SYSTEM "image/gif">

<!ENTITY mymovie SYSTEM "mymovie.mpeg" NDATA mpeg>
<!NOTATION mpeg SYSTEM "video/mpeg">

<!ENTITY mysound SYSTEM "mysound.wav" NDATA wav>
<!NOTATION wav SYSTEM "audio/x-wav">

<!ENTITY mypdf1 SYSTEM "mypdf.pdf" NDATA pdf>
<!ENTITY mypdf2 SYSTEM "mypdf.pdf" NDATA pdf>
<!NOTATION pdf SYSTEM "application/pdf">
```

Notice in the example above that both <!ENTITY> declarations with PDF content refer to the same notation – multiple unparsed entity declarations can use the same notation to describe their data.

Once an unparsed entity has been defined in the DTD, together with a notation that describes its content data, it can be embedded in the XML document by assigning it to an element attribute.

The <!ATTLIST> attribute declaration should include the 'ENTITY' keyword to denote that the attribute value will be an entity. The name given to an unparsed entity can then be assigned to that attribute and so embed the unparsed content in the XML document.

The XML document below embeds some of the unparsed entities, which are defined in the DTD, in the attributes of its <item> element. Disappointingly, at the time of writing, Internet Explorer is not yet able to use content embedded in XML documents:

ndata.xml

```
<?xml version="1.0" encoding="UTF-8"?>
<!DOCTYPE root SYSTEM "ndata.dtd" [
  <!ELEMENT root (item)*>
  <!ELEMENT item EMPTY>

  <!ATTLIST item pic ENTITY #IMPLIED>
  <!ATTLIST item mov ENTITY #IMPLIED>
  <!ATTLIST item pdf ENTITY #IMPLIED>
]>

<root>
  <item pic="mypic" />
  <item mov="mymovie" />
  <item pdf="mypdf1" />
</root>
```

Remember that XML's main task is to tag data – expect more capability to be added in the future.

```
<?xml version="1.0" encoding="UTF-8" ?>
<!DOCTYPE root (View Source for full doctype...)>
- <root>
    <item pic="mypic" />
    <item mov="mymovie" />
    <item pdf="mypdf1" />
  </root>
```

Done   My Computer

DTD modelling

You should now, hopefully, have an understanding of how to define rules for elements, attributes and entities that may appear in a XML document. This should enable you to start writing your own simple DTD.

The Open Applications Group is a good starting point when looking for a DTD – find them at:

www.openapplications.org

For a more complex DTD, it is worth considering if you can use one of the many existing DTDs that are available already. Try searching on the Internet for a similar application to your own. You may find one that almost suits your requirements and, because XML is extensible, can be adapted for you purposes quite easily.

There are a number of DTD modelling tools available that use the tree object model to simplify the creation of more complex DTDs. Each element is considered to be an object and the nesting relationship between the objects can be drawn diagrammatically and infinitely modified. When you are satisfied with the design the modelling tool will generate the final text-based DTD document.

XMLSpy contains a DTD design feature, that is worthy of investigation, but for a dedicated modelling tool try the Near & Far Designer from Microstar (**www.microstar.com**) shown below:

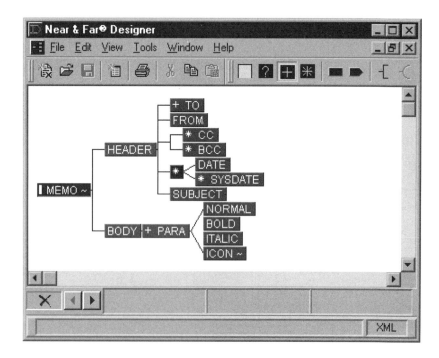

XMLSchema simple types

This chapter introduces the XMLSchema language which can be used in place of a DTD to define rules for XML documents. All the examples in this chapter demonstrate how single elements are defined as XMLSchema simple types.

Covers

Chapter Four

XMLSchema versus DTD

Schema rules written as a traditional DTD work well enough, but the newer XMLSchema language provides several improvements that allow the schema to have greater control with more flexibility:

- DTD syntax is not directly part of the XML language so DTD declarations cannot be processed by the XML parser.

  XMLSchema is itself written in XML so its schemas can be processed by the XML parser.

- All declarations in a DTD schema are global, so they will apply to the entire XML document. This means that you cannot declare two elements with the same name, even if they appear in different contexts within the document.

  XMLSchema allows you to specify global elements for the entire document and also local elements that can be used in different ways according to the document context where they appear.

- A DTD schema cannot specify what type of data an element may contain.

  XMLSchema provides a way to specify the type of data an element may contain. For instance, you can specify that an element should only contain an integer, another should only contain a string, another should only contain a date, and so on.

XMLSchema language was specifically developed by the World Wide Web Consortium (W3C) to meet the needs of XML.

The final point in the comparison above is the most marked difference between the two systems and allows XMLSchema much more control over element content than a DTD schema.

Any schema element declaration can be one of two types – those which can contain only text are a 'simple type', and those which can contain other elements, or have attributes, are a 'complex type'.

This chapter will illustrate how to start writing a schema using the XMLSchema language and explore XMLSchema simple type elements with particular emphasis on the ability to specify their content data type. XMLSchema complex type elements are discussed separately in the next chapter.

Beginning XMLSchema

XMLSchema documents simply state the schema rules for a XML document in plain text and have a **.xsd** file extension.

As XMLSchema is written in the XML language each schema document must begin with the standard XML declaration:

```
<?xml version="1.0" ?>
```

Like all XML documents the schema document must have a root element. Typically the schema root element is called 'xs:schema', where 'xs:' stands for 'XML Schema' and 'schema' defines that element as a schema declaration.

The XMLSchema language itself has a schema that is located at **http://www.w3.org/2001/XMLSchema**. This URL should be used in the XMLSchema document declaration to define it as the schema for the XMLSchema document. Typically the URL is assigned to 'xmlns:xs', where 'xmlns:' stands for 'XML Namespace' and 'xs' refers to the namespace prefix of that document.

More detail on the use of XML namespaces can be found in Chapter 6.

Once this declaration has been made, elements that are defined with the prefix 'xs:' will be recognised as belonging to this declared namespace.

So the start of a XMLSchema document might look like this:

```
<?xml version="1.0" encoding="UTF-8"?>

<xs:schema
    xmlns:xs="http://www.w3.org/2001/XMLSchema" >

    (schema rules are added here)

</xs:schema>
```

There is no absolute requirement to name the prefix 'xs:' and you may use any prefix you choose, so long as it is used consistently throughout the schema. The examples given in this book do, however, keep the 'xs:' prefix throughout, to avoid confusion.

Annotating comments

It is good practice to add comments to your code so that it can be more easily understood by others, or when revisiting the code.

The XMLSchema language provides three elements that can be used to annotate your schema code for clarity. The first one defines the general annotation section and is actually called 'annotation'. This would be added to the schema prefix to look like this:

```
<xs:annotation>          </xs:annotation>
```

The annotation element may optionally contain a child element called 'documentation', that is used to add human-readable text comments to a XMLSchema document. A further child element called 'appinfo' may also optionally be included in the annotation element to provide machine-readable information, such as a URL.

Both of these child elements may contain an attribute called 'source' to which a URL can be assigned.

Annotation can be added immediately after the 'xs:schema' element to provide information about the entire XMLSchema document. Also, annotation could be added after an individual element to provide information about that element.

Adding textual document annotation to a basic XMLSchema document would make it look like this:

```
<?xml version="1.0" encoding="UTF-8"?>
<xs:schema
    xmlns:xs="http://www.w3.org/2001/XMLSchema" >

<xs:annotation>
  <xs:documentation>
    The rules in this schema will be used to validate
    the content of a XML document.
  </xs:documentation>
</xs:annotation>
<xs:appinfo source="http://www.details"> </xs:appinfo>

    (schema rules are added here)

</xs:schema>
```

The XMLSchema declaration

The declaration of the XMLSchema schema that is to be used with a XML document is made in the root element of the XML document. This is unlike the DTD declaration that has a separate <!DOCTYPE> element for that purpose.

Target namespaces are explained in Chapter 6.

An attribute called 'xmlns:xsi' must first be added to the root element, where 'xmlns' stands for 'XML Namespace' and 'xsi:' stands for 'XMLSchema Instance'. This is assigned a URL of **http://www.w3.org/2001/XMLSchema-instance** that makes special elements available to specify the location of the schema for that document.

Many XML documents may include something called a 'target namespace' in the schema declaration but those that don't can indicate the location of their schema by assigning its URL to a special element called 'xsi:noNamespaceSchemaLocation'.

The schema example on this page gives a sneak preview of element declaration in XMLSchema documents.

The URL of the schema location can be stated as an absolute address, such as **http://www.domain/fruit.xsd**, if the schema is in a remote location. Alternatively, the location can be stated as a relative address, **fruit.xsd** like the example below that recreates the DTD example on page 35 using XMLSchema:

fruit.xml

```xml
<?xml version="1.0" encoding="UTF-8"?>
<fruit
   xmlns:xsi="http://www.w3.org/2001/XMLSchema-instance"
   xsi:noNamespaceSchemaLocation="fruit.xsd">

   <apple>Golden delicious</apple>
</fruit>
```

fruit.xsd

```xml
<?xml version="1.0" encoding="UTF-8"?>
<xs:schema xmlns:xs="http://www.w3.org/2001/XMLSchema">
   <xs:element name="fruit">
     <xs:complexType>
       <xs:sequence>
         <xs:element name="apple" type="xs:string"/>
       </xs:sequence>
     </xs:complexType>
   </xs:element>
</xs:schema>
```

Defining XMLSchema elements

An element is declared in a XMLSchema document using the element that is itself called 'element'. This is added after the schema's declared namespace prefix, for instance 'xs:element'.

The element declaration assigns a chosen name to its 'name' attribute, like this:

```
<xs:element name="apple" />
```

 A valid element name must start with a letter or underscore, that may then be followed by additional letters, numbers, underscores, hyphens or periods.

Whatever value has been assigned to the name attribute will specify how the tag will appear in the XML document. So a name value of 'apple' would represent a XML <apple> element tag.

An element is considered to be a simple type if it may only contain text, and so does not allow other elements or any attributes.

For simple type elements, XMLSchema provides a large number of built-in data types that can be used to specify allowable content. The data type is assigned to a 'type' attribute inside the element declaration to specify which type of data the element may contain.

When using built-in data types, the data type name should follow the declared schema prefix. This is needed because the data types are supplied to the schema namespace from the document's own schema at **http://www.w3.org/2001/XMLSchema**.

For an element that may contain a 'string' data type, consisting of letters, numbers or symbols, the element's type attribute could be assigned like this:

```
<xs:element name="apple" type="xs:string" />
```

This would allow the XML document to use the following element and content:

```
<apple>Golden delicious</apple>
```

An element that may contain an 'integer' data type, consisting of positive or negative whole numbers, could be assigned like this:

```
<xs:element name="quantity" type="xs:integer" />
```

The XML tag and content for this element might look like this:

```
<quantity>500</quantity>
<!-- or with a negative value -->
<quantity>-500</quantity>
```

An element that may contain a 'boolean' data type, which could be either true or false, or alternatively 1 or 0, can be assigned like this:

```
<xs:element name="status" type="xs:boolean" />
```

The XML tag and content for this element might look like this:

Note that a complete list of all built-in data types can be found at (no spaces):

http://www.w3.org/TR/xmlschema-2/#built-in-datatypes

```
<status>true</status>
<!-- or numerically 1=true 0=false -->
<status>1</status>
```

An element that may contain a 'date' data type, which must be in the format of CCYY-MM-DD, could be assigned like this:

```
<xs:element name="lunar-landing" type="xs:date" />
```

These examples show just some of the built-in data types that are available in the XMLSchema language.

The more commonly used data types are examined in closer detail over the next few pages.

The XML tag and content for this element might look like this:

```
<!-- The day the Eagle landed on the moon -->
<lunar-landing>1969-7-20</lunar-landing>
```

An element that may only contain a 'language' data type, that is an ISO two-letter country abbreviation, can be assigned like this:

```
<xs:element name="lang" type="xs:language" />
```

The XML tag and content for this element might look like this:

```
<!-- En Français -->
<lang>FR</lang>
```

Number types

XMLSchema provides a whole range of number data types that can be used to control the allowable content of a XML element.

The 'integer' data type allows zero and positive or negative whole numbers. This can be limited though by using the 'positiveInteger' data type instead to allow only positive whole numbers above zero. To allow only positive whole numbers including zero you can use the 'nonNegativeInteger' data type.

Similarly, the 'negativeInteger' data type only allows negative whole numbers below zero but the 'nonPositiveInteger' data type allows only negative whole numbers including zero.

For numbers that will contain a decimal point you can specify the 'decimal' data type that allows positive or negative numbers and zero. This should be used where the total number of digits is less than 18, counting those on both sides of the decimal point.

More precise decimal numbers can be allowed by specifying the 'float' data type that provides for single precision 32-bit floating point numbers. For even longer decimal numbers specify the 'double' data type to allow double precision 64-bit numbers. Both of these data types allow zero, and positive and negative numbers.

The schema fragment below declares elements using some of the data types on this page:

```
<xs:element name="int" type="xs:integer" />
<xs:element name="pos" type="xs:positiveInteger" />
<xs:element name="neg" type="xs:nonPositiveInteger" />
<xs:element name="dec" type="xs:decimal" />
<xs:element name="flt" type="xs:float" />
```

XML tags and content for these elements might look like this:

```
<int>123</int>    <int> -123</int>   <int>0</int>
<pos>123</pos>    <!-- but not 0 or -123 -->
<neg> -123</neg>  <neg>0</neg>   <!-- but not 123 -->
<dec>12345.67890</dec> <dec> -12345.67890</dec>
<flt>0.1234567890123456789012345678</flt>
```

Date and time types

A wide range of data types is available in XMLSchema to specify allowable content as a date, a time, or a period of time.

Date content is specified with the 'date' data type that requires the date to be in the backwards format of CCYY-MM-DD. For instance, '2003-02-21' represents 21st February, 2003.

Time content is specified with the 'time' data type that requires the time to be in the usual 24-hour format of hh:mm:ss. Optionally the time can add a timezone suffix. This uses the letter Z to indicate UTC (Greenwich Mean Time), or can use either +hh:mm or -hh:mm to indicate the difference from UTC.

The date and time can be combined in the single 'dateTime' data type that has the format CCYY-MM-DDThh:mm:ss and can also have the optional timezone indicators added.

If only a year is to be allowed you can use the 'gYear' data type that requires the CCYY format. The year and month can be allowed with the 'gYearMonth' data type that uses CCYY-MM formatting. Similarly, month and day is allowed with the 'gMonthDay' data type using the --MM-DD format and to allow only the day use the 'gDay' data type that needs the format of ---DD.

A duration of time can be specified with the 'duration' data type that has a specific format of PnYnDTnHnMnS. The letter P, for period, is always required and the letter T begins the optional time section. Each n indicates the number of Years, Months, Days, Hours, Minutes or Seconds in the total duration.

'Little Boy' was the nickname of the bomb dropped on Hiroshima at 8.15 a.m. on 6th August 1945. The Iditarod is a sled race across Alaska that was won recently in a time of 9 days 19 hours 55 minutes and 50 seconds.

```
<xs:element name="NYtime" type="xs:time" />
<xs:element name="littleBoy" type="xs:dateTime" />
<xs:element name="xmas" type="xs:gMonthDay" />
<xs:element name="iditarod" type="xs:duration" />
```

XML content for the above elements might look like this:

```
<NYtime>21:30:00-05:00</NYtime> <!-- UTC -5 hours -->
<littleBoy>1945-08-06T08:15:00</littleBoy>
<xmas>--12-25</xmas>
<iditarod>P9DT19H55M50S</iditarod>
```

Custom data types

The term given to the schema element that imposes the restriction is 'constraining facet'.

More of the XMLSchema constraining facets are examined over the next few pages.

The built-in data types in XMLSchema can be used as a base from which to create your own custom data types. A separate section of code, normally at the start of the schema, is used to define the custom data type so it can be used when defining elements later.

A custom data type definition should first have a name assigned to the 'name' attribute of an element called 'simpleType'. This element contains a child element called 'restriction' that has an attribute called 'base'. The built-in data type that is to be used as the basis of the custom data type is assigned to this attribute.

XMLSchema provides a number of constraining facet elements that can be nested inside the restriction element to shape the custom data type. One of these is the 'maxInclusive' constraining facet that has a 'value' attribute to which a maximum permissible numeric value can be assigned.

The schema shown on the right defines a custom data type called 'below100', that is subsequently used when declaring a XML element called <qty>, to only allow integer values up to 100.

```xml
<?xml version="1.0" encoding="UTF-8"?>
<xs:schema xmlns:xs="http://www.w3.org/2001/XMLSchema">

<xs:simpleType name="below100">
  <xs:restriction base="xs:integer">
    <xs:maxInclusive value="100"/>
  </xs:restriction>
</xs:simpleType>

<xs:element name="root">
  <xs:complexType>
    <xs:sequence>
      <xs:element name="qty" type="below100" />
    </xs:sequence>
  </xs:complexType>
</xs:element>
</xs:schema>
```

```xml
<root>
 <qty>50</qty> <!-- numbers over 100 are invalid -->
<root>
```

Range restriction

There are four constraining facets that can specify an allowable range when creating a custom data type. The top of the range can be fixed with either 'maxInclusive' or 'maxExclusive'. Using maxInclusive will allow up to, and including, the number assigned to the value attribute whereas maxExclusive only allows up to the assigned number -1.

The bottom of the range can be fixed with 'minInclusive' and 'minExclusive' which behave in the same way.

One of the max facets and one of the min facets are included in the custom data type definition to specify the range.

Range restrictions can be applied to dates and times, as well as numbers. Later dates or times are greater in the range, earlier ones are lower in the range.

The schema shown below sets a range restricting allowable times from midday until one second before midnight:

 It is useful to restrict date ranges so that an erroneous date cannot be used in a XML element.

```xml
<?xml version="1.0" encoding="UTF-8"?>
<xs:schema xmlns:xs="http://www.w3.org/2001/XMLSchema">

<xs:simpleType name="afternoon">
  <xs:restriction base="xs:time">
    <xs:maxInclusive value="23:59:59"/>
    <xs:minInclusive value="12:00:00"/>
  </xs:restriction>
</xs:simpleType>

<xs:element name="root">
  <xs:complexType>
    <xs:sequence>
      <xs:element name="pm" type="afternoon" />
    </xs:sequence>
  </xs:complexType>
</xs:element>
</xs:schema>
```

```xml
<root>
  <pm>15:00:00</pm> <!-- 00:00:00-11:59:59 is invalid -->
<root>
```

Restricting string length

The allowable length of a string in a XML element can be specified by creating a custom data type, based on a string data type, that uses 'minLength' and 'maxLength' constraining facets.

These will each have a number assigned to their value attribute to specify a minimum and maximum allowable string length.

This custom data type can then be assigned to the type attribute in the element declaration to restrict the size of string.

The schema below restricts the allowable length of a string to a range of between seven and ten characters:

```xml
<?xml version="1.0" encoding="UTF-8"?>
<xs:schema xmlns:xs="http://www.w3.org/2001/XMLSchema">

<xs:simpleType name="post-code">
  <xs:restriction base="xs:string">
    <xs:minLength value="7"/>
    <xs:maxLength value="10"/>
  </xs:restriction>
</xs:simpleType>

<xs:element name="root">
  <xs:complexType>
    <xs:sequence>
      <xs:element name="postcode" type="post-code"/>
    </xs:sequence>
  </xs:complexType>
</xs:element>
</xs:schema>
```

```xml
<root>
  <postcode>BS99 2PJ</postcode> <!-- valid length -->
<root>
```

Alternatively you can use a 'length' restriction element to specify an exact string length. For instance, we could replace the <xs:minLength> and <xs:maxLength> elements in the example above with <xs:length value="8"/> to specify that a valid string must be exactly 8 characters long.

Restricting digits

The allowable number of digits, on each side of a decimal point, can be specified by creating a custom numeric data type that uses 'fractionDigits' and 'totalDigits' constraining facets. The custom data type can be based on the decimal data type or any other numeric data type.

Whatever number is assigned to the value attribute of the fractionDigits facet will specify the allowable number of digits that may appear to the right of the decimal point.

Greater digit control can be gained using restriction patterns – for more details see overleaf.

The number assigned to the value attribute of the totalDigits facet will specify the total number of digits that may appear in the number, including both sides of the decimal point.

This offers less control than is first apparent because the number of allowable integer digits increases as the number of fractional digits diminishes. For instance, with a custom decimal-based data type, if you specify a fractionDigits value of 2 and a totalDigits value of 5, then 123.45, 1234.5 and 12345 would all be valid content.

The content values in this example could appear in the <number> element of a XML document using this schema:

```
<?xml version="1.0" encoding="UTF-8"?>
<xs:schema xmlns:xs="http://www.w3.org/2001/XMLSchema">
  <xs:simpleType name="num">
    <xs:restriction base="xs:decimal">
      <xs:fractionDigits value="2"/>
      <xs:totalDigits value="5"/>
    </xs:restriction>
  </xs:simpleType>

  <xs:element name="root">
    <xs:complexType>
      <xs:sequence>
        <xs:element name="number" type="num"/>
      </xs:sequence>
    </xs:complexType>
  </xs:element>
</xs:schema>
```

Restriction patterns

A pattern of allowable content can be specified as a regular expression in a 'pattern' constraining facet of a custom data type definition. The described pattern will determine what may be allowed in a XML element of this pattern type.

The topic of regular expressions is vast and fills entire books by itself. If you are familiar with the Perl language you are probably acquainted with regular expressions already. For those who are new to regular expressions, the table below gives an indication of the syntax used to describe allowable patterns:

Discover more about Perl and regular expressions in 'CGI & Perl in easy steps'.

\d	Any digit
\D	Anything except a digit
\s	Any whitespace – space, tab, newline or return
\S	Anything except whitespace
x*	Zero or multiple x characters
(xy)*	Zero or multiple xy characters
x?	One x character
(xy)?	One xy character
x+	One or more x characters
(xy)+	One or more xy characters
[xyz]	One group of xyz values
[0-9]	Any number from 0 to 9
x | y | z	Either x or y or z value
x{3}	Exactly 3 x characters in succession
x{3,}	At least 3 x characters
x{3,5}	At least 3, and at most 5, x characters
(xyz){3}	Exactly 3 xyz characters in succession

Regular expressions in XMLSchema are simplified so that parentheses enclose the pattern's characters, and curly brackets enclose an integer that is the number of times those characters should appear in the pattern.

For instance, a pattern of '1(\d){3}' would allow any number that begins with a one and is followed by three other digits.

The schema below specifies a pattern, in a constraining facet, that will allow only decimal numbers with 3 digits to the left of the decimal point and 2 digits to its right:

pattern.xsd

```xml
<?xml version="1.0" encoding="UTF-8"?>
<xs:schema xmlns:xs="http://www.w3.org/2001/XMLSchema">
  <xs:simpleType name="num">
    <xs:restriction base="xs:decimal">
      <xs:pattern value="(\d){3}(.){1}(\d){2}"/>
    </xs:restriction>
  </xs:simpleType>

  <xs:element name="root">
    <xs:complexType>
      <xs:sequence>
        <xs:element name="number" type="num"/>
      </xs:sequence>
    </xs:complexType>
  </xs:element>

</xs:schema>
```

pattern.xml

```xml
<?xml version="1.0" encoding="UTF-8" ?>
- <root
    xmlns:xsi="http://www.w3.org/2001/XMLSchema-instance"
    xsi:noNamespaceSchemaLocation="pattern.xsd">
    <number>964.25</number>
  </root>
```

Done   My Computer

Creating list data types

To allow XML elements to contain a list of items, a 'list' custom data type can be established in the schema. Each item in the list must be of the specified data type and each item must be separated from the next by whitespace.

The following schema creates a custom data type called 'dates'. This is then assigned to the type attribute in the <birthdays> element declaration to allow it to contain a list of dates:

Dates in the element must be in the valid format of CCYY-MM-DD.

```xml
<?xml version="1.0" encoding="UTF-8"?>
<xs:schema xmlns:xs="http://www.w3.org/2001/XMLSchema">

  <xs:simpleType name="dates">
    <xs:list itemType="xs:date"/>
  </xs:simpleType>

  <xs:element name="root">
    <xs:complexType>
      <xs:sequence>
        <xs:element name="birthdays" type="dates"/>
      </xs:sequence>
    </xs:complexType>
  </xs:element>

</xs:schema>
```

Constraints can be placed on the number of items that a list may contain by using the 'length', 'minLength' or 'maxLength' facets.

The 'datelist' code is to be added to the schema between the <xs:schema> tags – it does not replace other code.

The custom data type called 'datelist', which is created in the following schema fragment, is based on the 'dates' data type in the schema above but now restricts the list to allow just three items. Adding this code to the schema above will allow the 'datelist' data type to be assigned to the type attribute in the <birthdays> element declaration, so the element may only contain three dates:

```xml
<xs:simpleType name="datelist">
  <xs:restriction base="dates">
    <xs:length value="3"/>
  </xs:restriction>
</xs:simpleType>
```

Anonymous custom data types

Although the custom data type examples so far have all been named, it is not absolutely essential. If the purpose of the custom data type is solely to define a single element, it may be created within the <xs:element> </xs:element> tags. This means that it need not be named, as the cross-reference between the element and the custom data type is no longer required.

The schema below uses this method to create the <birthdays> element that can contain a list of three dates. This is more compact than the method used on the facing page, but is less clear and does not allow the custom data type to be reused:

dates.xsd

```
<?xml version="1.0" encoding="UTF-8"?>
<xs:schema xmlns:xs="http://www.w3.org/2001/XMLSchema">
  <xs:element name="root">
    <xs:complexType>
      <xs:sequence>
        <xs:element name="birthdays" >
          <xs:simpleType>
            <xs:restriction>
              <xs:simpleType>
                <xs:list itemType="xs:date"/>
              </xs:simpleType>
              <xs:length value="3"/>
            </xs:restriction>
          </xs:simpleType>
        </xs:element>
      </xs:sequence>
    </xs:complexType>
  </xs:element>
</xs:schema>
```

Valid content for the <birthdays> element might look like this:

dates.xml

```
<?xml version="1.0" encoding="UTF-8"?>
<root
   xmlns:xsi="http://www.w3.org/2001/XMLSchema-instance"
   xsi:noNamespaceSchemaLocation="dates.xsd">
<birthdays>1992-04-22 1994-07-11 1996-10-03</birthdays>
</root>
```

Stating acceptable values

A set of acceptable values can be specified in a custom data type by a number of 'enumeration' constraining facets. This custom data type can then be assigned to an element declaration type attribute to state a series of acceptable values that it may contain.

The schema below allows a XML element called <country> to contain any of the enumerated country names if they are identical in terms of capitalisation and whitespace:

Content of 'denmark' would be invalid because of incorrect capitalisation. Content of 'UnitedKingdom' would be invalid because of the omitted space.

```
<xs:schema xmlns:xs="http://www.w3.org/2001/XMLSchema">

<xs:simpleType name="europe">
  <xs:restriction base="xs:string">
    <xs:enumeration value="Austria"/>
    <xs:enumeration value="Belgium"/>
    <xs:enumeration value="Denmark"/>
    <xs:enumeration value="Finland"/>
    <xs:enumeration value="France"/>
    <xs:enumeration value="Germany"/>
    <xs:enumeration value="Greece"/>
    <xs:enumeration value="Ireland"/>
    <xs:enumeration value="Italy"/>
    <xs:enumeration value="Luxembourg"/>
    <xs:enumeration value="Netherlands"/>
    <xs:enumeration value="Portugal"/>
    <xs:enumeration value="Spain"/>
    <xs:enumeration value="Sweden"/>
    <xs:enumeration value="United Kingdom"/>
  </xs:restriction>
</xs:simpleType>

<xs:element name="root">
  <xs:complexType>
    <xs:sequence>
      <xs:element name="country" type="europe"/>
    </xs:sequence>
  </xs:complexType>
</xs:element>

</xs:schema>
```

XMLSchema complex types

This chapter adds to the introduction of the XMLSchema language in the previous chapter by demonstrating advanced features. All the examples in this chapter illustrate how elements that contain other elements, or that have attributes, are defined as XMLSchema complex types.

Covers

Chapter Five

Defining complex type elements

A complex type element may be considered to be one of four kinds according to the content that it contains:

- The 'element-only' kind may have attributes and will contain other elements, but will not contain any text. The element called <author> in the XML sample below is an element-only kind:

```
<author>
  <name>Mike McGrath</name>
</author>
```

- The 'empty' kind may have attributes but will not contain any text or other elements. This XML <tel> element is an empty element kind that has an attribute called 'number':

```
<tel number="555-1234" />
```

- The 'text-only' kind may contain attributes and will contain text, but will not contain other elements. The <colour> element in the XML sample below is a text-only element kind that has an attribute called 'favourite':

```
<colour favourite="true" />Green</colour>
```

- The 'mixed-content' kind may contain attributes, text and other elements. In the XML sample below, the <quote> element is a mixed-content element kind that contains text, another element called <literal>, and an attribute called 'src':

```
<quote src="Maréchal Pétain">
<literal lang="FR">Ils ne passeront pas</literal>
They shall not pass
</quote>
```

Notice the capitalisation of the term 'complexType', and note that it does not contain a space.

Each kind of complex type is demonstrated in this chapter.

All complex types are defined in a XMLSchema 'complexType' element and their name is assigned to its 'name' attribute. All the allowable content for that element is defined between the element's tags.

All elements that are defined within a XMLSchema complexType element must be part of either a sequence, a choice, an unordered group, or a named group. An example of each of these is demonstrated over the next few pages.

XMLSchema element names always follow the defined document namespace prefix – "xs:" in this example schema.

It is important to understand the distinction between 'definition' and 'declaration'. A complex type definition specifies allowable content, but it is only when the type is assigned in an element declaration that the definition is actually used.

The XMLSchema element shown below illustrates element tags for a complex type element called <info>:

```
<xs:complexType name="info">

    (content definitions are added here)

</xs:complexType>
```

Element definitions that are part of a sequence, can only appear in a XML document in the same order in which they have been defined. The complexType schema element that defines a sequence of allowable elements should contain its element definitions in a pair of XMLSchema 'sequence' tags.

The following schema creates a complex type called 'info' that defines a sequence of allowable elements. This is then assigned to the type attribute in an element declaration that defines an element called 'shopper'. When <shopper> appears in a XML document it must contain the defined elements, in the correct order:

```
<?xml version="1.0" encoding="UTF-8"?>
<xs:schema xmlns:xs="http://www.w3.org/2001/XMLSchema">

<!-- define a complex type called 'info'-->
<xs:complexType name="info">

  <!-- define the allowable elements as a sequence -->
  <xs:sequence>

    <!-- define the allowable elements -->
    <xs:element name="lastname" type="xs:string"/>
    <xs:element name="spend" type="xs:decimal"/>

  </xs:sequence>
</xs:complexType>

<!-- declare an element of the 'info' type -->
<xs:element name="shopper" type="info" />

</xs:schema>
```

Allowing element choice

A complex type can specify a choice of allowable elements using a XMLSchema 'choice' element to contain all the element definitions. The complex type can then be assigned to a type attribute in an element declaration. This will allow any *one* of the choice elements to appear once within the XML element.

The following schema defines a complex type called 'lang' that allows a choice of elements. This is then assigned to the type attribute in an element declaration for an element called 'language'. When <language> appears in a XML document it may contain either one <english> element, or one <german> element:

For details on how to allow multiple occurrences of any element see page 75.

```
<?xml version="1.0" encoding="UTF-8"?>
<xs:schema xmlns:xs="http://www.w3.org/2001/XMLSchema">

<!-- create a complex type element called 'lang' -->
<xs:complexType name="lang">

  <!-- declare the allowable elements to be a choice -->
  <xs:choice>

    <!-- define the allowable elements -->
    <xs:element name="english" type="xs:string"/>
    <xs:element name="german" type="xs:string"/>

  </xs:choice>
</xs:complexType>

<!-- declare an element of the 'lang' type -->
<xs:element name="language" type="lang"/>

</xs:schema>
```

Either, but not both, of the elements below could appear nested inside the <language> element tags in a XML document:

```
<german> Wer nicht liebt Wein, Weib und Gesang
         Der bleibt ein Narr sein Leben lang. </german>
```

```
<english> Who loves not woman, wine and song
          Remains a fool his whole life long. </english>
```

Allowing elements in any order

A complex type can define a set of allowable elements using a XMLSchema 'all' element to contain all the element definitions. The complex type can then be assigned to a type attribute in an element declaration. This will allow each of the elements in the set to appear once within the XML element *in any order*.

The following schema defines a complex type called 'hue' that allows a set of elements. This is then assigned to the type attribute in an element declaration for an element called 'colour'. When <colour> appears in a XML document it must contain one <red> element, one <green> element, and one <blue> element, but these may appear in any order:

colour.xsd

```xml
<?xml version="1.0" encoding="UTF-8"?>
<xs:schema xmlns:xs="http://www.w3.org/2001/XMLSchema">
  <xs:complexType name="hue">
    <xs:all>
      <xs:element name="red" type="xs:string"/>
      <xs:element name="green" type="xs:string"/>
      <xs:element name="blue" type="xs:string"/>
    </xs:all>
  </xs:complexType>
<xs:element name="colour" type="hue"/>
</xs:schema>
```

colour.xml

```
C:\MyXML\colour.xml
File   Edit   View   Favorites   Tools   Help

   <?xml version="1.0" encoding="UTF-8" ?>
 - <colour
     xmlns:xsi="http://www.w3.org/2001/XMLSchema
     -instance"
     xsi:noNamespaceSchemaLocation="colour.xsd">
     <green>Startling lime</green>
     <blue>Pacific blue</blue>
     <red>Flaming tomato</red>
   </colour>

Done                                    My Computer
```

Grouping elements

Elements can be grouped together with the XMLSchema element called 'group'. This is useful when elements appear together in different parts of a XML document because they can be referred to collectively using their group name.

The code fragment below shows the beginning of a schema called **stock.xsd** that first creates a group called 'product'. This allows either an element called <product-code>, or an element called <stock-number>, to be followed by an element called <price>:

top of stock.xsd

```xml
<?xml version="1.0" encoding="UTF-8"?>
<xs:schema xmlns:xs="http://www.w3.org/2001/XMLSchema">

  <xs:group name="product">
    <xs:sequence>
      <xs:choice>
        <xs:element name="product-code" type="xs:string"/>
        <xs:element name="stock-number" type="xs:string"/>
      </xs:choice>
      <xs:element name="price" type="xs:decimal"/>
    </xs:sequence>
  </xs:group>
```

A group can be referenced by assigning its name to a 'ref' attribute in a XMLSchema 'group' element. The **stock.xsd** schema uses the 'product' group in defining complex types 'general' and 'audio':

middle of stock.xsd

```xml
<xs:complexType name="general">
  <xs:sequence>
    <xs:element name="name" type="xs:string"/>
    <xs:group ref="product" />
  </xs:sequence>
</xs:complexType>

<xs:complexType name="audio">
  <xs:sequence>
    <xs:element name="title" type="xs:string"/>
    <xs:element name="artist" type="xs:string"/>
    <xs:group ref="product" />
  </xs:sequence>
</xs:complexType>
```

The 'general' complex type also defines an element called 'name', and the 'audio' complex type defines further elements called 'title' and 'artist'.

A further complex type can be created to define the allowable elements that may appear nested within the root element of the XML document. As this complex type will only be used with the root element it need not be named but can, instead, be included between the tags that declare the root element.

The **stock.xsd** schema declares a root <stock> element that can contain a <toy> element of the 'general' type, followed by a <cd> element of the 'audio' type:

bottom of stock.xsd

```
<xs:element name="stock">
  <xs:complexType>
    <xs:sequence>
      <xs:element name="toy" type="general" />
      <xs:element name="cd" type="audio" />
    </xs:sequence>
  </xs:complexType>
</xs:element>
</xs:schema>
```

stock.xml

The XML document can have a choice, defined in the group, between the <product-code> and <stock-number> elements.

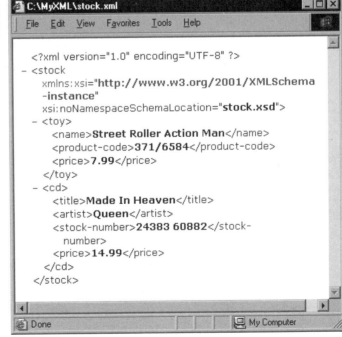

```
<?xml version="1.0" encoding="UTF-8" ?>
- <stock
    xmlns:xsi="http://www.w3.org/2001/XMLSchema
    -instance"
    xsi:noNamespaceSchemaLocation="stock.xsd">
  - <toy>
      <name>Street Roller Action Man</name>
      <product-code>371/6584</product-code>
      <price>7.99</price>
    </toy>
  - <cd>
      <title>Made In Heaven</title>
      <artist>Queen</artist>
      <stock-number>24383 60882</stock-number>
      <price>14.99</price>
    </cd>
  </stock>
```

Referencing elements

Both simple type and complex type elements that are declared just within the `<xs:schema>` tags are available globally across the schema. They can be referenced by assigning their name to a 'ref' attribute in an element declaration. It is especially useful to reference a complex type element that appears in several parts of the schema.

The schema below declares a simple type element called 'title' and a complex type element called 'detail'. Each of these is then included, by reference, in the definition of another complex type called 'list'. Finally, the schema declares a `<movie>` element of the 'list' type:

A globally declared element can only be referenced in sequences, choices, unordered group or named group definitions.

```xml
<?xml version="1.0" encoding="UTF-8"?>
<xs:schema xmlns:xs="http://www.w3.org/2001/XMLSchema">

  <!-- declare a simple type element -->
  <xs:element name="title" type="xs:string"/>

  <!-- declare a complex type element -->
  <xs:element name="detail">
    <xs:complexType>
      <xs:sequence>
        <xs:element name="format" type="xs:string"/>
        <xs:element name="price" type="xs:decimal"/>
      </xs:sequence>
    </xs:complexType>
  </xs:element>

  <!-- define a complex type -->
  <xs:complexType name="list">
    <xs:sequence>
      <!-- reference existing element declarations -->
      <xs:element ref="title"/>
      <xs:element ref="detail"/>
    </xs:sequence>
  </xs:complexType>

  <!-- declare an element of the defined complex type -->
  <xs:element name="movie" type="list"/>

</xs:schema>
```

Elements that are not declared globally cannot be referenced.

Controlling element occurrences

The attributes 'minOccurs' and 'maxOccurs' can be used to specify how many times an element, sequence, set of choices, unordered group or named group may appear. As their names suggest, they will respectively set the minimum and maximum number of allowable occurrences.

minOccurs and maxOccurs can only be used in local element declarations, and references to globally declared elements – not in actual global declarations.

The value assigned to the attribute will specify the number of allowable occurrences and can be any positive integer. Also maxOccurs can be assigned the keyword 'unbounded' to allow unlimited occurrences. Assigning a value of '0' to minOccurs in an element declaration effectively makes that element optional. The default value of each attribute is '1' unless an alternative value is specified.

The following schema declares a root element called <pets> containing string elements called <dog> and <cat>. The <dog> element may appear 1, 2 or 3 times. The <cat> element may appear once only, or may be omitted entirely:

pets.xsd

```xml
<?xml version="1.0" encoding="UTF-8"?>
<xs:schema xmlns:xs="http://www.w3.org/2001/XMLSchema">

  <xs:element name="pets">
    <xs:complexType>
      <xs:sequence>
<xs:element name="dog" type="xs:string" maxOccurs="3"/>
<xs:element name="cat" type="xs:string" minOccurs="0"/>
      </xs:sequence>
    </xs:complexType>
  </xs:element>

</xs:schema>
```

pets.xml

```xml
<?xml version="1.0" encoding="UTF-8"?>
<pets
    xmlns:xsi="http://www.w3.org/2001/XMLSchema-instance"
    xsi:noNamespaceSchemaLocation="pets.xsd">

  <dog>German Shepherd</dog>
  <dog>Labrador</dog>
</pets>
```

Text-only elements with attributes

An element without attributes that can only contain text should be defined as a simple type, but if the element is required to contain attributes it must be defined as a complex type.

The complex type can be based on any of the XMLSchema types, such as 'string' or 'integer'. The complex type defines the element type by assignation to the 'base' attribute of a XMLSchema element called 'extension'.

The 'number' attribute in this example is defined as a string type to allow hyphens to be included in the assigned value.

An attribute is defined with the XMLSchema element called 'attribute', that itself has a descriptive 'name' and 'type' attribute. Single, or multiple, attribute elements may be nested within a pair of 'extension' element tags.

The entire definition is contained in a XMLSchema 'simpleContent' element, that is nested within the 'complexType' tags, to denote that the allowable content is of simple type.

This schema defines a complex type that allows text content and has two attributes called 'name' and 'number':

item.xsd

```xml
<?xml version="1.0" encoding="UTF-8"?>
<xs:schema xmlns:xs="http://www.w3.org/2001/XMLSchema">
  <xs:complexType name="info">
    <xs:simpleContent>
      <xs:extension base="xs:string">
        <xs:attribute name="name" type="xs:string"/>
        <xs:attribute name="number" type="xs:string"/>
      </xs:extension>
    </xs:simpleContent>
  </xs:complexType>
  <xs:element name="item" type="info"/>
</xs:schema>
```

item.xml

```xml
<?xml version="1.0" encoding="UTF-8"?>
<item
  xmlns:xsi="http://www.w3.org/2001/XMLSchema-instance"
  xsi:noNamespaceSchemaLocation="item.xsd"
  name="Java 2 in easy steps" number="1-84078-025-8">
Learn how to program in Java.
</item>
```

Empty elements with attributes

An element declaration that does not assign any data type to its 'type' attribute will be considered to be an empty element that cannot contain data. These empty elements will always have attributes, otherwise their existence would be meaningless.

The schema below allows the root element to contain a string type element called <book>, and an empty element called <info> that contains two string type attributes:

books.xsd

The schema's <xs:sequence> element assigns an 'unbounded' value to its maxOccurs attribute to allow limitless occurrences of the sequence in the XML document.

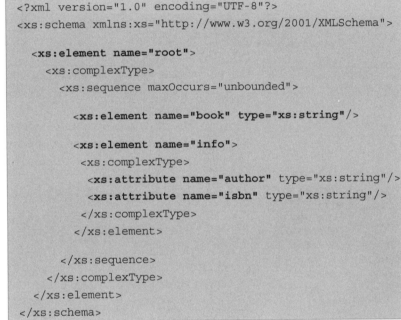

```xml
<?xml version="1.0" encoding="UTF-8"?>
<xs:schema xmlns:xs="http://www.w3.org/2001/XMLSchema">

  <xs:element name="root">
    <xs:complexType>
      <xs:sequence maxOccurs="unbounded">

        <xs:element name="book" type="xs:string"/>

        <xs:element name="info">
          <xs:complexType>
            <xs:attribute name="author" type="xs:string"/>
            <xs:attribute name="isbn" type="xs:string"/>
          </xs:complexType>
        </xs:element>

      </xs:sequence>
    </xs:complexType>
  </xs:element>
</xs:schema>
```

books.xml

```xml
<?xml version="1.0" encoding="UTF-8"?>
<root
  xmlns:xsi="http://www.w3.org/2001/XMLSchema-instance"
  xsi:noNamespaceSchemaLocation="books.xsd">

<book>CGI &apos; Perl in easy steps</book>
<info author="Mike McGrath" isbn="1-84078-027-4"/>

<book>HTML 4 in easy steps</book>
<info author="Mike McGrath" isbn="1-84078-048-7"/>

</root>
```

Mixed-content elements

A XMLSchema 'complexType' element can optionally include an attribute called 'mixed'. This can be assigned a 'true' value to allow that element to contain a mixture of other elements, attributes and text content.

In the following schema, mixed content is allowable in the <root> element. This may be limitless occurrences of a string type element called <heading>, and/or limitless occurrences of an element called <shape> with attributes of 'size' and 'colour':

shape.xsd

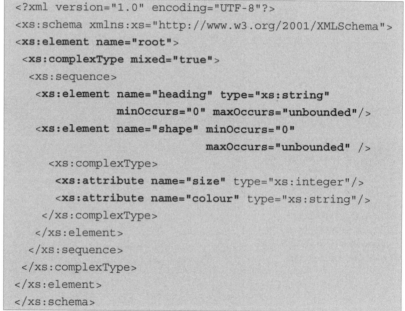

```
<?xml version="1.0" encoding="UTF-8"?>
<xs:schema xmlns:xs="http://www.w3.org/2001/XMLSchema">
<xs:element name="root">
 <xs:complexType mixed="true">
  <xs:sequence>
   <xs:element name="heading" type="xs:string"
               minOccurs="0" maxOccurs="unbounded"/>
   <xs:element name="shape" minOccurs="0"
                           maxOccurs="unbounded" />
    <xs:complexType>
     <xs:attribute name="size" type="xs:integer"/>
     <xs:attribute name="colour" type="xs:string"/>
    </xs:complexType>
   </xs:element>
  </xs:sequence>
 </xs:complexType>
</xs:element>
</xs:schema>
```

Using the minOccurs and maxOccurs attributes in this way means that the elements can appear limitless times, or may even be omitted.

shape.xml

```
<?xml version="1.0" encoding="UTF-8"?>
<root
   xmlns:xsi="http://www.w3.org/2001/XMLSchema-instance"
   xsi:noNamespaceSchemaLocation="shape.xsd">

<heading>Imagination and shapes</heading>

It is surprising how one circle
<shape size="3" colour="red"/>
may represent a snooker ball, but another circle
<shape size="7" colour="yellow"/> can resemble the sun.
</root>
```

Requiring attributes

By default any attribute is optional, so it can be either included in the XML element tag or omitted entirely. This optional use can be controlled though, by adding a 'use' attribute to the defining XMLSchema 'attribute' element.

The schema can then specify that a XML tag must always contain the attribute by assigning a value of 'required' to the 'use' attribute. Other possible values include 'optional', which is the default value in any event, or 'prohibited' to disallow the valid inclusion of an attribute:

The 'required' value is by far the one most used – the other values 'optional' and 'prohibited' are seldom found.

```
<?xml version="1.0" encoding="UTF-8"?>
<xs:schema xmlns:xs="http://www.w3.org/2001/XMLSchema">

  <xs:complexType name="product">
    <xs:simpleContent>
      <xs:extension base="xs:string">
        <xs:attribute name="code" type="xs:string"
                                      use="required"/>
        <xs:attribute name="weight" type="xs:string"
                                      use="optional"/>
        <xs:attribute name="colour" type="xs:string"
                                      use="prohibited"/>
      </xs:extension>
    </xs:simpleContent>
  </xs:complexType>

  <xs:element name="root">
    <xs:complexType>
      <xs:sequence minOccurs="0" maxOccurs="unbounded">
        <xs:element name="phone" type="product"/>
      </xs:sequence>
    </xs:complexType>
  </xs:element>
</xs:schema>
```

A XML document using the schema shown above could contain limitless occurrences of a <phone> element which must each have a 'code' attribute. They may also, optionally, contain a 'weight' attribute, but they cannot contain a 'colour' attribute.

Grouping attributes

If a set of attributes will appear in more than one definition it is a good idea to create a group for them. The group can then be efficiently referenced from each definition to incorporate those attributes. This avoids the need to repeat the full attribute code on each occasion.

The schema that follows first defines an attribute group called 'info' containing attributes of 'filetype', 'width' and height':

top of images.xsd

```
<?xml version="1.0" encoding="UTF-8"?>
<xs:schema xmlns:xs="http://www.w3.org/2001/XMLSchema">

  <!-- define an attribute group -->
  <xs:attributeGroup name="info">
    <xs:attribute name="filetype" type="xs:string"/>
    <xs:attribute name="width" type="xs:integer"/>
    <xs:attribute name="height" type="xs:integer"/>
  </xs:attributeGroup>
```

Complex types called 'static' and 'motion' are then defined which reference the attribute group to incorporate its attributes. The 'motion' definition also adds a further attribute called 'runtime':

middle of images.xsd

```
  <!-- define a complex type for static images -->
  <xs:complexType name="static">
    <xs:simpleContent>
      <xs:extension base="xs:string">
        <xs:attributeGroup ref="info"/>
      </xs:extension>
    </xs:simpleContent>
  </xs:complexType>

  <!-- define a complex type for motion images -->
  <xs:complexType name="motion">
    <xs:simpleContent>
      <xs:extension base="xs:string">
        <xs:attributeGroup ref="info"/>
        <xs:attribute name="runtime" type="xs:string"/>
      </xs:extension>
    </xs:simpleContent>
  </xs:complexType>
```

Now that all definitions are made, the elements are declared. The <root> element is allowed to contain a static type <image> element, and a <video> motion type element:

bottom of images.xsd

```
<!-- declare all elements -->
<xs:element name="root">
  <xs:complexType>
    <xs:sequence>
      <xs:element name="image" type="static"
                  minOccurs="0" maxOccurs="unbounded"/>
      <xs:element name="video" type="motion"
                  minOccurs="0" maxOccurs="unbounded"/>
    </xs:sequence>
  </xs:complexType>
</xs:element>

</xs:schema>
```

images.xml

The minOccurs and maxOccurs attribute values allow unlimited numbers of either element to be used.

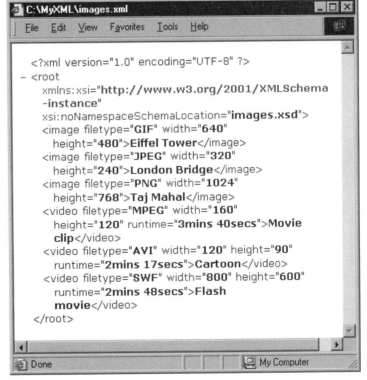

```
C:\MyXML\images.xml
File  Edit  View  Favorites  Tools  Help

<?xml version="1.0" encoding="UTF-8" ?>
- <root
    xmlns:xsi="http://www.w3.org/2001/XMLSchema
    -instance"
    xsi:noNamespaceSchemaLocation="images.xsd">
  <image filetype="GIF" width="640"
    height="480">Eiffel Tower</image>
  <image filetype="JPEG" width="320"
    height="240">London Bridge</image>
  <image filetype="PNG" width="1024"
    height="768">Taj Mahal</image>
  <video filetype="MPEG" width="160"
    height="120" runtime="3mins 40secs">Movie
    clip</video>
  <video filetype="AVI" width="120" height="90"
    runtime="2mins 17secs">Cartoon</video>
  <video filetype="SWF" width="800" height="600"
    runtime="2mins 48secs">Flash
    movie</video>
</root>

Done                          My Computer
```

Predefining attribute values

Allowable XML element attribute values can be specified by adding 'fixed' or 'default' attributes to the XMLSchema 'attribute' element. This schema assigns values to both:

packet.xsd

```xml
<?xml version="1.0" encoding="UTF-8"?>
<xs:schema xmlns:xs="http://www.w3.org/2001/XMLSchema">
  <xs:complexType name="data">
    <xs:simpleContent>
      <xs:extension base="xs:string">
        <xs:attribute name="code"   type="xs:integer"
                                          default="12345"/>
          <xs:attribute name="weight" type="xs:string"
                                          fixed="100g"/>

      </xs:extension>
    </xs:simpleContent>
  </xs:complexType>
  <xs:element name="root">
    <xs:complexType>
      <xs:sequence minOccurs="0" maxOccurs="unbounded">
        <xs:element name="packet" type="data"/>
      </xs:sequence>
    </xs:complexType>
  </xs:element>
</xs:schema>
```

You can ensure an attribute must be present in an element by adding use='required' – see page 79.

packet.xml

If present, an attribute with a fixed value ('weight' in this case) must contain that value. An attribute with a default value ('code' in this case) may be assigned a different value.

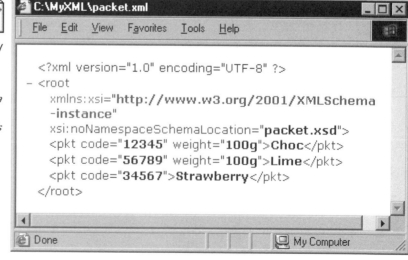

```
C:\MyXML\packet.xml

File   Edit   View   Favorites   Tools   Help

  <?xml version="1.0" encoding="UTF-8" ?>
- <root
    xmlns:xsi="http://www.w3.org/2001/XMLSchema
    -instance"
    xsi:noNamespaceSchemaLocation="packet.xsd">
    <pkt code="12345" weight="100g">Choc</pkt>
    <pkt code="56789" weight="100g">Lime</pkt>
    <pkt code="34567">Strawberry</pkt>
  </root>

Done                                    My Computer
```

Anonymous complex type elements

For complex types that will not be reused, it is often more efficient to define an un-named complex type within an element declaration. The schema on the facing page has been modified like this in the example below that incorporates the second complex type definition within the root element declaration:

object2.xsd

```xml
<?xml version="1.0" encoding="UTF-8"?>
<xs:schema xmlns:xs="http://www.w3.org/2001/XMLSchema">

  <!-- 1st complex type with 1 element + 1 attribute -->
  <xs:complexType name="obj">
    <xs:simpleContent>
      <xs:extension base="xs:string">
        <xs:attribute name="colour" type="xs:string"/>
      </xs:extension>
    </xs:simpleContent>
  </xs:complexType>

  <!-- declare root element with 2nd complex type-->
  <xs:element name="root">
    <!-- 2nd complex type with 1st type + 2 elements -->
    <xs:complexType>
      <xs:sequence>
        <xs:element name="object" type="obj"/>
        <xs:element name="width" type="xs:decimal"/>
        <xs:element name="height" type="xs:decimal"/>
      </xs:sequence>
    </xs:complexType>
  </xs:element>

</xs:schema>
```

It is simply a matter of taste whether you use the more modular approach taken by the schema on the opposite page, or if you prefer the more compact approach of the schema on this page.

object2.xml

```xml
<?xml version="1.0" encoding="UTF-8"?>
<root
    xmlns:xsi="http://www.w3.org/2001/XMLSchema-instance"
    xsi:noNamespaceSchemaLocation="object2.xsd">
<object colour="gold">Rectangle</object>
<width>24.0</width> <height>12.0</height>
</root>
```

Complex types in other complex types

Once a complex type has been defined it can be included in other complex type definitions:

object.xsd

The example schema on the right defines a first complex type that has one element with a single attribute. A second complex type definition has an element of the first complex type, and adds two further elements.

Finally, the <root> element is declared as a second complex type to allow the XML document to contain all three elements.

```xml
<?xml version="1.0" encoding="UTF-8"?>
<xs:schema xmlns:xs="http://www.w3.org/2001/XMLSchema">

  <!-- 1st complex type with 1 element + 1 attribute -->
  <xs:complexType name="obj">
    <xs:simpleContent>
      <xs:extension base="xs:string">
        <xs:attribute name="colour" type="xs:string"/>
      </xs:extension>
    </xs:simpleContent>
  </xs:complexType>

  <!-- 2nd complex type with 1st type + 2 elements -->
  <xs:complexType name="dimension">
    <xs:sequence>
      <xs:element name="object" type="obj"/>
      <xs:element name="width" type="xs:decimal"/>
      <xs:element name="height" type="xs:decimal"/>
    </xs:sequence>
  </xs:complexType>

  <!-- declare root element of the 2nd complex type -->
  <xs:element name="root" type="dimension"/>

</xs:schema>
```

object.xml

```xml
<?xml version="1.0" encoding="UTF-8"?>
<root
  xmlns:xsi="http://www.w3.org/2001/XMLSchema-instance"
  xsi:noNamespaceSchemaLocation="object.xsd">
<object colour="gold">Rectangle</object>
<width>24.0</width> <height>12.0</height>
</root>
```

XML namespaces

This chapter illustrates how a unique 'namespace' identifier can be associated with XMLSchema documents and XML documents. This is useful to guarantee the uniqueness of your documents in the distributed environment of the Internet.

Covers

Chapter Six

XMLSchema namespaces

A namespace is simply a way to uniquely identify the components of a XML document. In a XMLSchema document the default namespace is assigned to a 'xmlns' attribute in the root element of the document.

The assigned value should be a URL, although this is only used as a means to provide the document with a unique identifier.

The schema of XMLSchema language is sometimes called the 'schema for schemas'.

A XMLSchema document can assign the URL of the XMLSchema language's own schema to the 'xmlns' attribute, so that it becomes the default namespace for that document. The root element of a schema could then begin like this:

```
<schema xmlns="http://www.w3.org/2001/XMLSchema"
```

This means that all XMLSchema elements need not be prefixed when they appear in the schema. For instance, the tag to declare an element is simply <element>, rather than <xs:element>.

To allow the schema components to be uniquely identified a unique URL should also be assigned to the 'targetNamespace' attribute of the XMLSchema <schema> element. Typically this will be an address using your own domain name, so the root element of a schema could now begin like this:

```
<schema xmlns="http://www.w3.org/2001/XMLSchema"
    targetNamespace="http://www.ineasysteps.com/xml/ns"
```

For more on namespace URLs see page 96 at the end of this chapter.

Finally, a prefix needs to be defined that must be used when referring to the global components of the schema after they have been created. Choose a short prefix then add it after 'xmlns:' to form a special attribute, like 'xmlns:my'. The URL of the target namespace can then be assigned to it in the <schema> element.

A root element of a valid schema defining a default namespace, a target namespace and a namespace prefix could now look like this:

```
<schema xmlns="http://www.w3.org/2001/XMLSchema"
    targetNamespace="http://www.ineasysteps.com/xml/ns"
    xmlns:my="http://www.ineasysteps.com/xml/ns" >
</schema>
```

DTDs do not support namespaces – this is chiefly why many people prefer XMLSchema.

The XMLSchema example below demonstrates a valid XMLSchema document that uses a target namespace prefix called 'my'. Notice that the XMLSchema elements no longer have the 'xs:' prefix that has been used in the previous examples. Also take note that the complex type is defined as simply 'product', but is referred to as 'my:product' when it is assigned to the type attribute in the <root> element declaration:

phones.xsd

The namespace prefix is used with global components – not those local ones inside a complex type.

This schema is used to validate the example XML document that is shown on page 89.

```xml
<?xml version="1.0" encoding="UTF-8"?>

<schema
  xmlns="http://www.w3.org/2001/XMLSchema"
  targetNamespace="http://www.ineasysteps.com/xml/ns"
  xmlns:my="http://www.ineasysteps.com/xml/ns" >

<!-- define a complex type with 5 elements -->

<complexType name="product">
  <sequence>
    <element name="make" type="string"/>
    <element name="model" type="integer"/>
    <element name="code" type="string"/>
    <element name="grams" type="integer"/>
    <element name="price" type="decimal"/>
  </sequence>
</complexType>


<!-- declare a root element -->

<element name="root">
  <complexType>
    <sequence minOccurs="0" maxOccurs="unbounded">
      <element name="phone" type="my:product"/>
    </sequence>
  </complexType>
</element>

</schema>
```

XML document namespaces

A XML document that uses a XMLSchema document to validate its content will specify information about the schema in its root element opening tag.

This first assigns the URL of the XMLSchema-instance's own schema to the special attribute typically called 'xmlns:xsi':

```
xmlns:xsi="http://www.w3.org/2001/XMLSchema-instance"
```

This is much like defining a default namespace for the XML document.

A unique namespace that can be used to uniquely identify the components of your XML document is created by assigning a unique URL to a special attribute .

This comprises 'xmlns:' followed by a short prefix that you choose, for instance 'xmlns:my':

```
xmlns:my="http://www.ineasysteps.com/xml/ns"
```

Finally, the location of the actual XMLSchema document is specified by assigning the URL of the target namespace, together with the schema document file name, to an attribute called 'xsi:schemaLocation' in the root element:

The target namespace and the file name should be separated by whitespace when assigning the schema location.

```
xsi:schemaLocation=
"http://www.ineasysteps.com/xml/ns filename.xsd"
```

Because the root element is defined to be in a unique namespace it should now appear with the defined namespace prefix in the XML document.

A root element of a valid XML document that defines a namespace prefix, a default instance namespace and the location of a XMLSchema document, could look like this:

```
<root xmlns:my="http://www.ineasysteps.com/xml/ns"
xmlns:xsi="http://www.w3.org/2001/XMLSchema-instance"
xsi:schemaLocation="http://www.ineasysteps.com/xml/ns
schemafile.xsd" >
```

The example below illustrates a valid XML document that defines the standard XMLSchema-instance location, a unique namespace called 'my', and the location of its XMLSchema document that is to be used for validation of its content.

Notice that the root element must now appear as 'my:root' because it has been defined as belonging to the namespace:

phones.xml

Most of the data in this example could alternatively have been stated as attributes in the <phone> element. This option is the subject of much debate, but many consider it better to isolate data into separate elements as shown with this example.

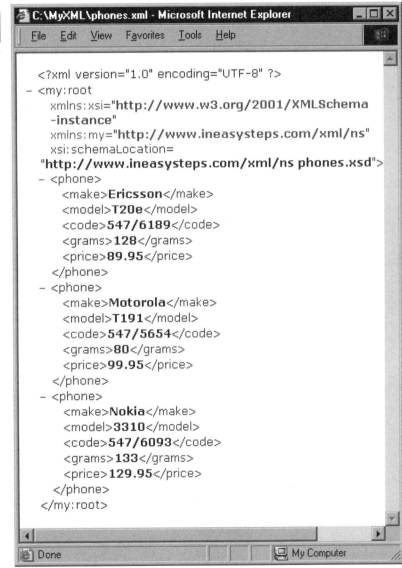

```xml
<?xml version="1.0" encoding="UTF-8" ?>
- <my:root
    xmlns:xsi="http://www.w3.org/2001/XMLSchema
    -instance"
    xmlns:my="http://www.ineasysteps.com/xml/ns"
    xsi:schemaLocation=
  "http://www.ineasysteps.com/xml/ns phones.xsd">
  - <phone>
      <make>Ericsson</make>
      <model>T20e</model>
      <code>547/6189</code>
      <grams>128</grams>
      <price>89.95</price>
    </phone>
  - <phone>
      <make>Motorola</make>
      <model>T191</model>
      <code>547/5654</code>
      <grams>80</grams>
      <price>99.95</price>
    </phone>
  - <phone>
      <make>Nokia</make>
      <model>3310</model>
      <code>547/6093</code>
      <grams>133</grams>
      <price>129.95</price>
    </phone>
  </my:root>
```

Qualifying elements and attributes

A XMLSchema can insist that the namespace prefix must be used with its elements and attributes when they appear in a XML document. All elements can be made to require the namespace prefix by assigning a value of 'qualified' to an attribute called 'elementFormDefault' in the XMLSchema's <schema> tag. Similarly, all attributes can be made to require the namespace prefix by assigning a value of 'qualified' to an attribute called 'attributeFormDefault' in the <schema> tag.

The other possible value for these attributes is 'unqualified' which is the default value that applies if the attribute is omitted.

Individual elements and attributes can be made to require the namespace prefix by adding a 'form' attribute to their declarations. This can be assigned a value of 'qualified' or 'unqualified' and will override any default that may have been set in the <schema> tag.

The following schema requires that all elements except <price> must appear in the XML document with the namespace prefix. No attributes are present but the attributeFormDefault is included in the <schema> tag for illustration purposes:

*top of
mobiles.xsd*

```
<?xml version="1.0" encoding="UTF-8"?>

<schema xmlns="http://www.w3.org/2001/XMLSchema"
    targetNamespace="http://www.ineasysteps.com/xml/ns"
    xmlns:my="http://www.ineasysteps.com/xml/ns"
    elementFormDefault="qualified"
    attributeFormDefault="unqualified" >

<!-- define complex type with 5 elements -->

<complexType name="product">
  <sequence>
    <element name="make" type="string"/>
    <element name="model" type="string"/>
    <element name="code" type="string"/>
    <element name="grams" type="integer"/>
    <element name="price" type="decimal"
                          form="unqualified"/>

  </sequence>
</complexType>
```

bottom of mobiles.xsd

```
<!-- declare root element with above complex type -->

  <element name="root">
    <complexType>
      <sequence minOccurs="0" maxOccurs="unbounded">
        <element name="phone" type="my:product"/>
      </sequence>
    </complexType>
  </element>

</schema>
```

A XML document that uses this schema must include the namespace prefix with every element except <price>:

mobiles.xml

Prefixes beginning with the three-letter sequence x, m, l, in any case combination, are reserved for use by XML and XML-related specifications.

```
C:\MyXML\mobiles.xml - Microsoft Internet Explorer

File   Edit   View   Favorites   Tools   Help

<?xml version="1.0" encoding="UTF-8" ?>
- <my:root
    xmlns:xsi="http://www.w3.org/2001/XMLSchema
    -instance"
    xmlns:my="http://www.ineasysteps.com/xml/ns"
    xsi:schemaLocation=
  "http://www.ineasysteps.com/xml/ns mobiles.xsd">
  - <my:phone>
    <my:make>Ericsson</my:make>
    <my:model>T20e</my:model>
    <my:code>547/6189</my:code>
    <my:grams>128</my:grams>
    <price>89.95</price>
  </my:phone>
  - <my:phone>
    <my:make>Motorola</my:make>
    <my:model>T191</my:model>
    <my:code>547/5654</my:code>
    <my:grams>80</my:grams>
    <price>99.95</price>
  </my:phone>
</my:root>

Done                                My Computer
```

Using multiple schemas

The components of a schema can be split across several schema documents to make their contents more modular. A XMLSchema 'include' element can make the contents of another schema available by assigning its URL to a 'schemaLocation' attribute inside the schema's include tag.

In the **telephones.xsd** schema below, the include element makes available the top-level components of a schema called **weight.xsd**. The included schema is shown on the facing page, and contains a complex type definition called 'weight-info'. This is assigned as the data type in the <weight> element declaration shown below:

telephones.xsd

Notice that the complex type from the included schema has the schema prefix 'my:' when it is assigned in the <weight> element declaration.

```xml
<?xml version="1.0" encoding="UTF-8"?>

<schema xmlns="http://www.w3.org/2001/XMLSchema"
   targetNamespace="http://www.ineasysteps.com/xml/ns"
   xmlns:my="http://www.ineasysteps.com/xml/ns"  >

   <!-- include schema for the weight complex type -->
   <include schemaLocation="weight.xsd"/>

   <!-- define complex type with 5 elements -->
   <complexType name="product">
     <sequence>
       <element name="make" type="string"/>
       <element name="model" type="string"/>
       <element name="code" type="string"/>
       <element name="weight" type="my:weight-info"/>
       <element name="price" type="decimal"/>
     </sequence>
   </complexType>

   <!-- declare root element with above complex type -->
   <element name="root">
     <complexType>
       <sequence minOccurs="0" maxOccurs="unbounded">
         <element name="phone" type="my:product"/>
       </sequence>
     </complexType>
   </element>

</schema>
```

The **weight.xsd** schema shown below simply defines a complex type called 'weight' that extends the string data type and contains a single attribute called 'units'. This schema is included in the schema on the opposite page:

weight.xsd

```
<?xml version="1.0" encoding="UTF-8"?>
<schema xmlns="http://www.w3.org/2001/XMLSchema"
targetNamespace="http://www.ineasysteps.com/xml/ns"
xmlns:my="http://www.ineasysteps.com/xml/ns" >

  <!-- define a string element with 1 attribute -->
  <complexType name="weight-info">
    <simpleContent>
      <extension base="string">
        <attribute name="units" type="integer" />
      </extension>
    </simpleContent>
  </complexType>
</schema>
```

This XML document conforms to the **telephones.xsd** schema:

telephones.xml

```
C:\MyXML\telephones.xml - Microsoft Internet Explorer
File  Edit  View  Favorites  Tools  Help

<?xml version="1.0" encoding="UTF-8" ?>
- <my:root
    xmlns:xsi="http://www.w3.org/2001/XMLSchema
    -instance"
    xmlns:my="http://www.ineasysteps.com/xml/ns"
    xsi:schemaLocation=
"http://www.ineasysteps.com/xml/ns telephones.xsd">
  - <phone>
      <make>Ericsson</make>
      <model>T20e</model>
      <code>547/6189</code>
      <weight units="grams">128</weight>
      <price>89.95</price>
    </phone>
  </my:root>

Done                                My Computer
```

Importing from other namespaces

Components can be imported into a schema from other schemas which have a different target namespace, using the XMLSchema 'import' element. This has an attribute called 'namespace' that should be assigned the target namespace that is used by the schema you wish to import from. A second attribute 'schemaLocation' is assigned the URL of the schema to be imported.

Once the import element has been added, along with its attributes, a new namespace prefix needs to declared in the <schema> tag so that the components in the imported schema can be referenced. The declaration adds the chosen prefix after 'xmlns:' to form a special attribute. This is then assigned the URL that is the target namespace used by the imported schema. Its components can then be referred to with the new prefix followed by their original name.

This is really the whole point of namespaces because it allows the re-use of components across documents without the problem of conflicting component names. The processor sees the name as being the combination of the prefix and the given name, thus ensuring that no two are identical.

The following schema simply defines a complex type that is imported by the schema on the opposite page. That schema is then used to validate the XML file at the bottom of the facing page:

mikes-schema.xsd

```
<?xml version="1.0" encoding="UTF-8"?>

<schema xmlns="http://www.w3.org/2001/XMLSchema"
   targetNamespace="http://www.mikes.com/xml/ns"
   xmlns:mike="http://www.mikes.com/xml/ns" >

   <!-- define a string element with 1 attribute -->

   <complexType name="phone-numbers">
     <simpleContent>
       <extension base="string">
         <attribute name="class" type="string"/>
       </extension>
     </simpleContent>
   </complexType>

</schema>
```

jeffs-schema.xsd

```xml
<?xml version="1.0" encoding="UTF-8"?>
<schema xmlns="http://www.w3.org/2001/XMLSchema"
  targetNamespace="http://www.jeffs.com/xml/ns"
  xmlns:jeff="http://www.jeffs.com/xml/ns"
  xmlns:mike="http://www.mikes.com/xml/ns" >

<!-- import a second schema  -->
<import namespace="http://www.mikes.com/xml/ns"
        schemaLocation="mikes-schema.xsd"/>

<!-- define a complex type with 3 elements -->
<complexType name="personal-info">
  <sequence>
    <element name="name" type="string"/>
    <element name="address" type="string"/>
    <element name="tel" type="mike:phone-numbers"
                        minOccurs="1" maxOccurs="5"/>
  </sequence>
</complexType>

<!-- declare root element with above complex type -->
<element name="root">
  <complexType>
    <sequence minOccurs="0" maxOccurs="unbounded">
      <element name="info" type="jeff:personal-info"/>
    </sequence>
  </complexType>
</element>
</schema>
```

This schema uses the 'mike:' prefix to refer to components in the imported schema and the 'jeff:' prefix to refer to components in this schema.

jeffs-doc.xml

```xml
<?xml version="1.0" encoding="UTF-8"?>
<jeff:root
  xmlns:xsi="http://www.w3.org/2001/XMLSchema-instance"
  xmlns:jeff="http://www.jeffs.com/xml/ns"
  xsi:schemaLocation=
        "http://www.jeffs.com/xml/ns jeffs-schema.xsd">
  <info>
    <name>Susan McGrath</name>
    <address>123 Anyplace, London</address>
    <tel class="home">555-9876</tel>
    <tel class="office">555-3456</tel>
    <tel class="mobile">555-1234</tel>
  </info>
</jeff:root>
```

Choosing a namespace name

In order to create a namespace name for your XML documents it is best to use your own domain name. If you do not currently have a domain name you may want to consider registering one so that you can uniquely identify the components in your documents.

Because the URL identifies the owner of the namespace you cannot use somebody else's domain as your namespace unless they have explicitly agreed to it. For instance, you could not use the URL of **http://www.ineasysteps.com/xml/ns** that is used in some of the examples given in this book.

For low prices try the domain registration service that is offered at:

www.123-reg.co.uk

The cost to register your own domain name is very inexpensive but does vary according to your choice of Top Level Domain (TLD). A '.com' domain will cost around £10 per year and a 'co.uk' domain will cost even less.

Do not be persuaded to register domain names in multiple TLDs as this is generally both unnecessary and expensive. There are already over 250 TLDs, with more being added all the time.

Some ISPs offer a 'domain parking' facility that can provide you with a unique domain name to use for your XML namespace at a nominal cost – ask your ISP, or try **www.freeparking.co.uk**.

When considering a name for a new domain, try to keep it as short as possible. This will pay dividends in the future by keeping the amount of typing to a minimum.

After registering a domain name, it will remain yours while you continue to pay the yearly charge. You can move to any other ISP and still keep your registered domain name.

A namespace is that part of a valid URL web address that does not specifically include a named file. Instead, it just indicates the possible location of a directory that may, or may not, actually exist.

It is a good idea to include a version number in the URL so that the namespace can be updated in the future, like these examples:

- http://domain/xml/ns/1.0

- http://www.w3.org/XSL.Transform/1.0

- http://www.w3.org/TR/REC-html40

XSL transformation

The eXtensible Stylesheet Language (XSL) has been developed to provide a means to transform and format the content of XML documents. It is split into two parts called XSLT (XSL Transformation) and XSL-FO (XSL Formatting Objects).

XSLT is explored in this chapter with demonstrations that transform XML into HTML pages for display in a browser. XSL-FO is not yet supported by browsers so currently XML is often formatted by Cascading Stylesheets (CSS) – see Chapter 9 for more information.

Covers

Chapter Seven

The node tree

The Microsoft XML parser includes a XSL processor. When the XSL processor analyses a XML document it breaks it into separate pieces called 'nodes'. Each node represents a part of the document, such as an element, an attribute or some text content. The nodes are established in their correct hierarchical order to form a 'node tree' of the entire document.

shoes.xml

```
<?xml version="1.0" encoding="UTF-8"?>
<products xsi:noNamespaceSchemaLocation="shoes.xsd"
    xmlns:xsi="http://www.w3.org/2001/XMLSchema-instance">
  <footwear>
    <make code="NIK1078">Nike</make>
    <model>Libretto</model>
    <price>49.99</price>
  </footwear>
</products>
```

The XML document above, is depicted by this node tree:

The Microsoft XML/XSL parser and processor is called 'MSXML' – for more details search for MSXML on the web at:

www.microsoft.com

When the processor has completed the node tree it will seek a XSLT style sheet for instructions on how to use the nodes. These instructions are contained within 'templates' in the style sheet.

The following pages in this chapter build a variety of example XSLT style sheets for the **shoes.xml** document shown above.

Beginning a XSLT style sheet

A XSLT style sheet states rules which govern how the content of a XML document should be handled. It is a plain text document that has a **.xsl** file extension.

As XSLT is written in the XML language, each XSLT style sheet must begin with the standard XML declaration:

```
<?xml version="1.0" encoding="UTF-8"?>
```

Like all XML documents, the style sheet must have a root element. Typically this is called 'xsl:stylesheet', where 'xsl:' stands for 'eXtensible Stylesheet Language' and 'stylesheet' indicates that the element is a style sheet declaration.

The declaration should assign a version number to a 'version' attribute – currently this is '1.0'. The XSLT schema location at **http://www.w3.org/1999/XSL/Transform** is assigned to create a default namespace. Typically the URL is assigned to 'xmlns:xsl', where 'xmlns:' stands for 'XML Namespace' and 'xsl' refers to the namespace prefix of that document.

Once this declaration has been made, elements that are declared with the prefix 'xsl:' will be recognised as belonging to this namespace.

So the start of a XSLT style sheet might look like this:

Do not leave a space between 'style' and 'sheet' in the element declaration 'xsl:stylesheet'.

```
<?xml version="1.0" encoding="UTF-8"?>

<xsl:stylesheet version="1.0"
    xmlns:xsl="http://www.w3.org/1999/XSL/Transform" >

    (style sheet rules are added here)

</xsl:stylesheet>
```

There is no absolute requirement to name the prefix 'xsl:' and you may use any prefix you choose, so long as it is used consistently throughout the style sheet. The examples given in this book do, however, keep the 'xsl:' prefix throughout, to avoid confusion.

The root template

After the XSL processor has established the node tree of a XML document it will look for a XSLT style sheet for instructions on how to use the nodes. These instructions are contained inside templates.

All HTML code that is within a XSLT style sheet must be well-formed.

The processor first seeks a template containing instructions that it can apply to the root node of the XML document. This is normally located immediately after the 'xsl:stylesheet' declaration and is declared in a XSLT element called 'xsl:template'. The element has an attribute called 'match' that can be assigned a '/', forward slash character, to denote a pattern that matches the root node of the XML document.

So a root element opening tag looks like this:

```
<xsl:template match="/">
```

The structure of the transformed output document is defined between the root element tags of a XSLT style sheet. For HTML output, this will include <html>, <head> and <body> tags plus other HTML tags to format content of the output document.

In the following XSLT style sheet the root element defines a simple HTML document containing a formatted text message:

shoes-1.xsl

```
<?xml version="1.0" encoding="UTF-8"?>
<xsl:stylesheet version="1.0"
    xmlns:xsl="http://www.w3.org/1999/XSL/Transform">

<xsl:template match="/">
 <html>
  <head>
    <title>Output document</title>
  </head>
  <body>
    <font size="6"><b>Hello from XSLT...</b></font>
  </body>
 </html>
</xsl:template>

</xsl:stylesheet>
```

Outputting HTML code

To associate a XSLT style sheet with a XML document there needs to be a processor instruction included to give its location. This is placed immediately after the standard processor instruction that is the usual XML declaration on the first line.

Processor instructions start with '<?' and end with '?>' and the instruction regarding a style sheet is called 'xml:stylesheet'. This includes a 'href' attribute, that is assigned the location of the style sheet, and a 'type' attribute, that is assigned the MIME type of the style sheet – for instance, 'text/xsl'.

A XML document using the XSLT style sheet on the facing page could look like this:

shoes.xml

```
<?xml version="1.0" encoding="UTF-8"?>
<?xml:stylesheet href="shoes-1.xsl" type="text/xsl"?>
<products xsi:noNamespaceSchemaLocation="shoes.xsd"
   xmlns:xsi="http://www.w3.org/2001/XMLSchema-instance">
  <footwear>
    <make code="NIK1078">Nike</make>
    <model>Libretto</model>
    <price>49.99</price>
  </footwear>
</products>
```

Opening the above XML document in Internet Explorer now applies the XSLT style sheet and produces the HTML output that is defined in its root element:

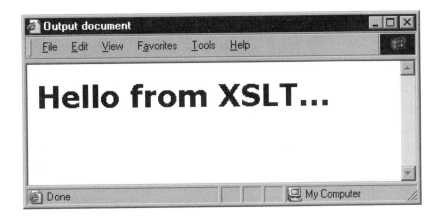

Outputting a node

A XSLT style sheet can include selected data from its associated XML document in the HTML output that it generates.

The node can be simply added in-line into the HTML code that is defined in the XSLT style sheet's root template. This requires the 'select' attribute of a XSLT element called 'xsl:value-of' to be assigned the tree location of the node.

A tree location is defined hierarchically starting from the root element and working through any child elements, using the syntax of 'parent/child/grandchild'.

It is important to note that only the value of the first node will be output from XML documents that contain multiple occurrences of the same node name. This is demonstrated by the following example that contains three occurrences of a node tree location of 'footwear/make' – only the content of the first is output.

The XML document below contains three sequences of elements with different content. An instruction on the second line tells the XSLT processor to use a style sheet called **shoes-2.xsl**, shown on the opposite page, to apply a transformation:

shoes.xml

```xml
<?xml version="1.0" encoding="UTF-8"?>
<?xml:stylesheet href="shoes-2.xsl" type="text/xsl"?>
<products
  xmlns:xsi="http://www.w3.org/2001/XMLSchema-instance"
  xsi:noNamespaceSchemaLocation="shoes.xsd">

  <footwear>
    <make code="NIK1078">Nike</make>
    <model>Libretto</model> <price>49.99</price>
  </footwear>
  <footwear>
    <make code="REE678">Reebok</make>
    <model>Classic Club</model> <price>29.99</price>
  </footwear>
  <footwear>
    <make code="ADI587">Adidas</make>
    <model>St.Kilda</model> <price>34.99</price>
  </footwear>
</products>
```

The XSLT style sheet shown below is called by the XSL processor when the XML document on the facing page is opened by Internet Explorer. It outputs three of the nodes from the XML code in the HTML page that is generated:

shoes-2.xsl

```
<?xml version="1.0" encoding="UTF-8"?>
<xsl:stylesheet version="1.0"
    xmlns:xsl="http://www.w3.org/1999/XSL/Transform">

<xsl:template match="/">

<html>
  <head>
    <title>Output document</title>
  </head>

  <body>
    <h2>Special Offers!</h2> <hr/>
    Great value on all our
    <xsl:value-of select="products/footwear/make"/>
    range of shoes today!<br/>
    The <xsl:value-of select="products/footwear/model"/>
    shoe is a great buy at just
    £<xsl:value-of select="products/footwear/price"/>
  </body>
</html>

</xsl:template>

</xsl:stylesheet>
```

Applying template rules

Style rules can be defined in templates to format selected elements within a XML document when they are output as HTML. The XSLT style sheet on the facing page is used by the XML document below to generate HTML output using four templates:

shoes.xml

```
<?xml version="1.0" encoding="UTF-8"?>
<?xml:stylesheet href="shoes-3.xsl" type="text/xsl"?>
<products
   xmlns:xsi="http://www.w3.org/2001/XMLSchema-instance"
   xsi:noNamespaceSchemaLocation="shoes.xsd">

  <footwear>
    <make code="NIK1078">Nike</make>
    <model>Libretto</model> <price>49.99</price>
  </footwear>
  <footwear>
    <make code="REE678">Reebok</make>
    <model>Classic Club</model> <price>29.99</price>
  </footwear>
  <footwear>
    <make code="ADI587">Adidas</make>
    <model>St.Kilda</model> <price>34.99</price>
  </footwear>
</products>
```

The individual 'xsl:template' definitions follow the root template. Each definition first assigns a value to its 'match' attribute to determine which XML element the template will apply to. Note that this is just the element's name, not its node tree address. In this example the first three templates apply to any element that match the assigned name. The fourth template will only apply to the element that matches the defined name and attribute value.

A single template can be applied by assigning its node tree address to a 'select' attribute in the 'xsl:apply-templates' tag. For instance, 'select="footwear/model"'.

The rules of how to treat the matched elements are contained between the 'xsl:template' tags. These each have an 'xsl:value-of' element which declares that the rule should be applied to the current node by assigning a '.' to their 'select' attribute.

The templates are applied by adding an 'xsl:apply-templates' element in the root template, so that any text or HTML code that is defined by the rule is added to each matching node.

shoes-3.xsl

```
<?xml version="1.0" encoding="UTF-8"?>
<xsl:stylesheet version="1.0"
    xmlns:xsl="http://www.w3.org/1999/XSL/Transform">

<xsl:template match="/">
<html><head><title>Output document</title></head>
<body>
<xsl:apply-templates />
</body></html>
</xsl:template>

<xsl:template match="make">
<b><xsl:value-of select="."/></b>
</xsl:template>

<xsl:template match="model">
<i> (<xsl:value-of select="."/>)</i>
</xsl:template>

<xsl:template match="price">
£<xsl:value-of select="."/><br/><br/>
</xsl:template>

<xsl:template match="make[@code='ADI587']">
<U><xsl:value-of select="."/></U>
</xsl:template>

</xsl:stylesheet>
```

Notice that the style sheet only applies the template that explicitly matches the third element – the text content 'Adidas' is underlined but is not displayed in bold text.

The content of <price> elements gain a '£' character and each <model> element is displayed in italic font within brackets. Generally each <make> element is displayed in bold but the one also matching the attribute is displayed with an underline:

Nike *(Libretto)* £49.99

Reebok *(Classic Club)* £29.99

<u>Adidas</u> *(St.Kilda)* £34.99

Done   My Computer

Creating HTML tables

The nature of the data stored in a XML document makes it often desirable to have a style sheet output its contents in tabular form. XSLT provides a 'xsl:for-each' element that makes this simple.

Multiple XML elements that have the same name can be considered to be a 'node set'. Each of the nodes in a set can be addressed in sequential order using the 'xsl:for-each' element.

The sample XML document 'shoes.xml' is also featured in other examples in this chapter. The only change is to the style sheet assigned to handle its content. This apparent repetition is to make each example complete for any readers who are dipping in and out of this book.

The XML document below uses the XSLT style sheet on the facing page to generate a HTML table that displays its contents. A template that matches with the root element first defines the top row of column headers in regular HTML. Next the 'xsl:for-each' element's 'select' attribute is assigned the parent of the nodes whose contents are to be listed by looping through the node set levels in sequence.

Each pass of the loop through the data builds a table row with content from each level of the node sets deposited in table cells. The output from this example is shown at the bottom of the facing page and includes a column featuring attribute values in addition to those with element text content:

shoes.xml

```
<?xml version="1.0" encoding="UTF-8"?>
<?xml:stylesheet href="shoes-4.xsl" type="text/xsl"?>
<products
    xmlns:xsi="http://www.w3.org/2001/XMLSchema-instance"
    xsi:noNamespaceSchemaLocation="shoes.xsd">

    <footwear>
        <make code="NIK1078">Nike</make>
        <model>Libretto</model> <price>49.99</price>
    </footwear>
    <footwear>
        <make code="REE678">Reebok</make>
        <model>Classic Club</model> <price>29.99</price>
    </footwear>
    <footwear>
        <make code="ADI587">Adidas</make>
        <model>St.Kilda</model> <price>34.99</price>
    </footwear>
</products>
```

shoes-4.xsl

The 'xsl:apply-templates' element includes the table in the HTML output that is defined in the root element.

Note the syntax that is used here to access the value of an attribute – 'element/@attribute'.

```xml
<?xml version="1.0"?>

<xsl:stylesheet version="1.0"
  xmlns:xsl="http://www.w3.org/1999/XSL/Transform">

<xsl:template match="/">
  <html> <head> <title>Output document</title> </head>
  <body> <xsl:apply-templates /> </body> </html>
</xsl:template>

<xsl:template match="products">
  <table width="100%" border="2">
    <tr bgcolor="silver">
      <td>Make</td>
      <td>Code</td>
      <td>Model</td>
      <td>Price</td>
    </tr>

    <xsl:for-each select="footwear">
      <tr>
        <td><xsl:value-of select="make"/></td>
        <td><xsl:value-of select="make/@code"/></td>
        <td><xsl:value-of select="model"/></td>
        <td><xsl:value-of select="price"/></td>
      </tr>
    </xsl:for-each>

  </table>
</xsl:template>

</xsl:stylesheet>
```

Make	Code	Model	Price
Nike	NIK1078	Libretto	49.99
Reebok	REE678	Classic Club	29.99
Adidas	ADI587	St.Kilda	34.99

Done   My Computer

Choices in templates

A template can apply different formatting to nodes depending upon the result of a stated conditional test within a template. The choices are stated in blocks of code between a pair of 'xsl:choose' tags and the conditional test is assigned to the 'test' attribute of a 'xsl:when' element. Whatever formatting is defined between these 'xsl:when' tags will only be applied to the node if the test is found to be true.

The expression to be tested is stated in the XPath language that is explored in Chapter 8. In this example the test will be true when the 'make' element's 'code' attribute matches the string.

The 'xsl:choose' element can contain multiple conditional tests in separate 'xsl:when' elements. Alternative formatting may be defined in a final 'xsl:otherwise' element that will only be applied when previous conditional tests fail.

The XSLT style sheet on the facing page is used by the XML document shown below. It makes conditional tests within two 'xsl:when' elements to see if the current node of an attribute matches a given string. When the attribute matches, the relevant formatting is applied, but when both tests fail the alternative in the 'xsl:otherwise' element is applied.

Opening this XML document with Internet Explorer produces the output illustrated at the bottom of the opposite page:

shoes.xml

```xml
<?xml version="1.0" encoding="UTF-8"?>
<?xml:stylesheet href="shoes-5.xsl" type="text/xsl"?>
<products
  xmlns:xsi="http://www.w3.org/2001/XMLSchema-instance"
  xsi:noNamespaceSchemaLocation="shoes.xsd">
  <footwear>
    <make code="NIK1078">Nike</make>
    <model>Libretto</model> <price>49.99</price>
  </footwear>
  <footwear>
    <make code="REE678">Reebok</make>
    <model>Classic Club</model> <price>29.99</price>
  </footwear>
  <footwear>
    <make code="ADI587">Adidas</make>
    <model>St.Kilda</model> <price>34.99</price>
  </footwear>
</products>
```

shoes-5.xsl

```xml
<?xml version="1.0" encoding="UTF-8"?>
<xsl:stylesheet version="1.0"
  xmlns:xsl="http://www.w3.org/1999/XSL/Transform">

<xsl:template match="/">
  <html> <head> <title>Output document</title> </head>
  <body> <h4> <u>Shoe Prices</u> </h4>
  <xsl:apply-templates /> </body> </html>
</xsl:template>

<xsl:template match="price">
  <xsl:choose>

    <xsl:when test="../make/@code='REE678'">
      <b> - sold out</b><br/>
    </xsl:when>

    <xsl:when test="../make/@code='ADI587'">
      <xsl:text> </xsl:text> <b>
      <xsl:value-of select="."/> -special offer</b><br/>
    </xsl:when>

    <xsl:otherwise>
      <b> £<xsl:value-of select="."/> </b><br/>
    </xsl:otherwise>

  </xsl:choose>
</xsl:template>

<xsl:template match="model">
  <i>...<xsl:value-of select="."/> </i>
</xsl:template>
</xsl:stylesheet>
```

HOT TIP

Notice the use of a 'xsl:text' element in the second test block to add a space into the formatting.

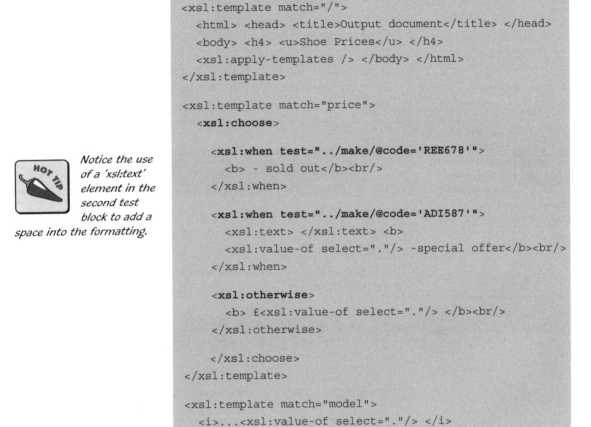

Shoe Prices

Nike...*Libretto* **£49.99**
Reebok...*Classic Club* - **sold out**
Adidas...*St.Kilda* **34.99 - special offer**

Done · My Computer

Sorting node output order

Nodes will normally be processed by a XSLT style sheet in the order which they appear in a XML document. They may, however, be sorted into a different order using a 'xsl:sort' element within a 'xsl:for-each' block of code.

The 'select' attribute of a 'xsl:sort' element must be assigned the name of a node set upon which to base the sorting order.

Sorting is carried out, by default, in ascending order from A–Z alphabetically and from the lowest number upwards numerically. This can be reversed by including an 'order' attribute in the 'xsl:sort' element, with an assigned value of 'descending'.

To omit the 'data-type' attribute, or to assign the wrong data type value, will lead to unpredictable results.

Specify the type of content to be sorted by assigning either 'text' or 'number' to the 'data-type' attribute of the 'xsl:sort' element. This determines whether to sort alphabetically or numerically.

The style sheet on the opposite page is used by the XML document below to rearrange its output in two different ways. It first sorts the nodes alphabetically, based on the document's <make> content. Then it sorts the nodes numerically, based on the document's <price> content:

shoes.xml

```
<?xml version="1.0" encoding="UTF-8"?>
<?xml:stylesheet href="shoes-6.xsl" type="text/xsl"?>
<products
  xmlns:xsi="http://www.w3.org/2001/XMLSchema-instance"
  xsi:noNamespaceSchemaLocation="shoes.xsd">

  <footwear>
    <make code="NIK1078">Nike</make>
    <model>Libretto</model> <price>49.99</price>
  </footwear>
  <footwear>
    <make code="REE678">Reebok</make>
    <model>Classic Club</model> <price>29.99</price>
  </footwear>
  <footwear>
    <make code="ADI587">Adidas</make>
    <model>St.Kilda</model> <price>34.99</price>
  </footwear>
</products>
```

shoes-6.xsl

```xml
<?xml version="1.0"?>
<xsl:stylesheet version="1.0"
  xmlns:xsl="http://www.w3.org/1999/XSL/Transform">

<xsl:template match="/">
<html> <head> <title>Output document</title> </head>
<body> <xsl:apply-templates /> </body> </html>
</xsl:template>

<xsl:template match="products">
  <b>Sorted alphabetically by make:</b><br/>
  <xsl:for-each select="footwear">
    <xsl:sort select="make"
              order="ascending" data-type="text"/>
    <xsl:value-of select="make"/> -
    <xsl:value-of select="model"/> -
    £<xsl:value-of select="price"/><br/>
  </xsl:for-each>

  <b>Sorted numerically by price:</b><br/>
  <xsl:for-each select="footwear">
    <xsl:sort select="price"
              order="ascending" data-type="number"/>
    <xsl:value-of select="make"/> -
    <xsl:value-of select="model"/> -
    £<xsl:value-of select="price"/><br/>
  </xsl:for-each>
</xsl:template>
</xsl:stylesheet>
```

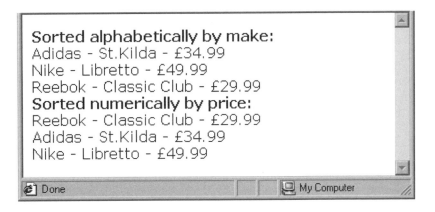

Sorted alphabetically by make:
Adidas - St.Kilda - £34.99
Nike - Libretto - £49.99
Reebok - Classic Club - £29.99
Sorted numerically by price:
Reebok - Classic Club - £29.99
Adidas - St.Kilda - £34.99
Nike - Libretto - £49.99

Done   My Computer

Generating HTML attributes

A XSLT style sheet can output HTML tags containing attributes using the 'xsl:attribute' element. More significantly, selected data in the XML document can be assigned to these attributes.

The attribute must first be named by assigning a name to the 'name' attribute of an opening 'xsl:attribute' element tag. The content between its tags will become the value assigned to that HTML attribute.

In this example the image file name is formed by a concat() function which is part of the XPath language – see Chapter 8.

The XSLT style sheet on the facing page is used by the XML document below to create valid HTML <img> tags that display images associated with each of its node levels. The images are all in the GIF file format and named with the code given to each shoe. The <make> element's code value is extracted by the template at each node level and is concatenated with the string '**.gif**' to make the full file name. This is assigned to the HTML 'src' attribute.

This template creates 'width' and 'height' attributes in the HTML <img> tag, to standardise the image size in the output. Also a HTML 'alt' attribute is added to the <img> tag and is assigned the value of the <model> element at each node level:

shoes.xml

```
<?xml version="1.0" encoding="UTF-8"?>
<?xml:stylesheet href="shoes-7.xsl" type="text/xsl"?>
<products
  xmlns:xsi="http://www.w3.org/2001/XMLSchema-instance"
  xsi:noNamespaceSchemaLocation="shoes.xsd">

  <footwear>
    <make code="NIK1078">Nike</make>
    <model>Libretto</model> <price>49.99</price>
  </footwear>
  <footwear>
    <make code="REE678">Reebok</make>
    <model>Classic Club</model> <price>29.99</price>
  </footwear>
  <footwear>
    <make code="ADI587">Adidas</make>
    <model>St.Kilda</model> <price>34.99</price>
  </footwear>
</products>
```

shoes-7.xsl

NIK1078.gif
REE678.gif
ADI587.gif

```xml
<?xml version="1.0"?>
<xsl:stylesheet version="1.0"
  xmlns:xsl="http://www.w3.org/1999/XSL/Transform" >

<xsl:template match="/">
  <html> <head> <title>Output document</title> </head>
  <body> <xsl:apply-templates/> </body> </html>
</xsl:template>

<xsl:template match="make">
  <img>
    <xsl:attribute name="src">
      <xsl:value-of select="concat( ./@code,'.gif' )"/>
    </xsl:attribute>
    <xsl:attribute name="width">130</xsl:attribute>
    <xsl:attribute name="height">68</xsl:attribute>
    <xsl:attribute name="alt">
      <xsl:value-of select="../model"/>
    </xsl:attribute>
  </img>
  <b><xsl:value-of select="."/></b>
</xsl:template>

<xsl:template match="price">
  <big><i>£<xsl:value-of select="."/></i></big> <hr/>
</xsl:template>

</xsl:stylesheet>
```

> **HOT TIP**
>
> Notice how the syntax '..' is used to refer to the parent of the node matched by a template.

The XSLT Designer

You can download a fully-featured evaluation copy of the XML Spy suite at:

www.xmlspy.com

The XML Spy IDE suite includes a program called XSLT Designer that can automatically generate a XSLT style sheet. It is supplied with a tutorial to get you started and is well worth examining.

To start using XSLT Designer, a schema needs to be loaded and a XML document assigned to provide working data. Specific schema elements can then be dragged from the left pane of the Designer window and dropped into the right pane, to build a style sheet.

The source code and browser preview can be seen at any time by clicking tabs at the bottom of the Designer window:

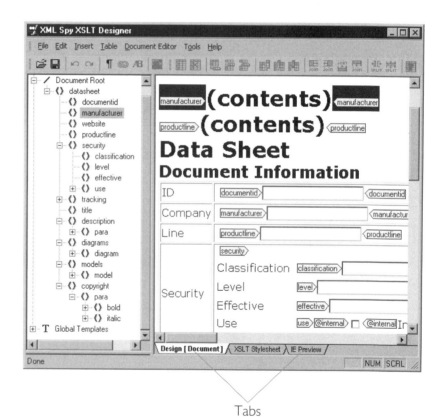

Tabs

XPath language

One or two features of the XML Path language (XPath) were included in a couple of examples in the previous chapter, but this chapter explores XPath in more detail. Examples illustrate how to use the XPath syntax to form patterns and expressions, and useful XPath functions are demonstrated.

Covers

Chapter Eight

What is XPath?

The XPath language provides syntax to address the nodes of a XML document tree by describing their hierarchical relationship. This form of address is similar to the composition of a URL.

XPath has functions which can be used to manipulate strings, numbers and boolean values, and XPath can also describe patterns which can be tested against a node for a match.

Expressions can be written using XPath syntax and are useful in XSLT when offering choices within templates. For instance, if an expression evaluated to a true value the template could apply certain formatting, otherwise it could apply alternative formatting.

The node tree of a XML document can contain different types of nodes, such as element nodes, attribute nodes and text nodes. XPath can address any one of these either absolutely, from the root element down, or relatively, from within a current node.

A XSLT template that matches 'size' in this example would apply its formatting rules to each of the 'size' nodes in that node set when called by an <xsl:apply-templates/> tag.

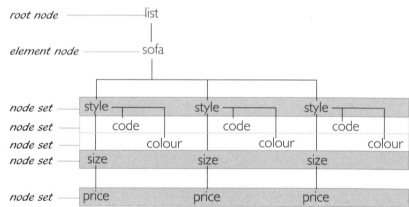

The node tree depicted above illustrates the element nodes and attribute nodes of the XML document that is used in this chapter. The full source code for this document, with comments, is shown on the opposite page. The root node 'list' contains a single child element called 'sofa' that contains three elements 'style', 'size' and 'price'. The 'style' element has attributes called 'code' and 'colour'.

It is important to understand the parent and child relationship between the nodes. For instance, the 'sofa' node is a child of 'list' and also the parent of 'style', 'size' and 'price'.

sofas.xml

This XML document is used by each of the XSLT style sheets examples given in this chapter. Only the style sheet file name assigned to its 'href' attribute is changed for each example.

For instance, the first example assigns **sofas-1.xsl**, the next example assigns **sofas-2.xsl**, and so on.

Remember to change the value assigned to the 'href' attribute in this example, from **sofas-0.xsl** to the file name of the appropriate style sheet.

```xml
<?xml version="1.0" encoding="UTF-8"?>

<!-- specify the appropriate XSLT style sheet -->
<?xml:stylesheet href="sofas-0.xsl" type="text/xsl"?>

<!-- root element specifying a validating schema -->
<list xsi:noNamespaceSchemaLocation="sofas.xsd"
  xmlns:xsi="http://www.w3.org/2001/XMLSchema-instance">

  <!-- complex type element with 3 element sequence -->
  <!-- 1st occurrence -->
  <sofa>

    <!-- complex type string element + 2 attributes -->
    <style code="S123" colour="red">Bali</style>

    <!-- simple type string element -->
    <size>3-seater</size>

    <!-- simple type decimal element -->
    <price>449.99</price>

</sofa>

  <!-- 2nd occurrence -->
  <sofa>
    <style code="S456" colour="green">Alto</style>
    <size>2-seater</size>
    <price>299.99</price>
  </sofa>

  <!-- 3rd occurrence -->
  <sofa>
    <style code="S789" colour="blue">Peru</style>
    <size>3-seater</size>
    <price>399.99</price>
  </sofa>

</list>
```

Addressing the current node

When a XSLT style sheet template is applied, the processor steps through the node tree seeking a match for the value assigned to its 'match' attribute. On finding a successful match, that node becomes the current node and the template executes its formatting instructions before continuing its search. The next match then becomes the current node, and so on.

The '.' syntax will be familiar to users of the old MS-DOS command line to mean 'current' location.

The absolute address of the matches would, of course, be different so it is not convenient to use absolute addressing within a XSLT template. Instead, the XPath syntax '.' can be used to address each node that is current at the time it is being processed by the template.

In the following style sheet, the template matches a <price> element node, so it becomes the current node and the formatting specified in the template is applied. This process is repeated for the other two <price> element nodes:

sofas-1.xsl

```
<?xml version="1.0"?>
<xsl:stylesheet version="1.0"
    xmlns:xsl="http://www.w3.org/1999/XSL/Transform" >

<xsl:template match="/">
  <html> <head> <title>Output document</title> </head>
  <body> <xsl:apply-templates/> </body> </html>
</xsl:template>

<xsl:template match="price">
   - <b>£<xsl:value-of select="."/></b><br/>
</xsl:template>

</xsl:stylesheet>
```

This output is generated by using the style sheet on this page with the XML document on page 117.

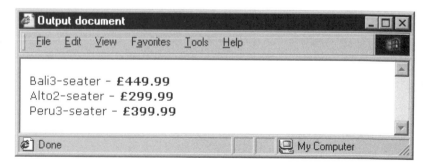

Output document

File　Edit　View　Favorites　Tools　Help

Bali3-seater - **£449.99**
Alto2-seater - **£299.99**
Peru3-seater - **£399.99**

Done　　　My Computer

Addressing child nodes

Child nodes represent those elements that are contained in the element that is represented by the current node.

You can address a grandchild of the current node using 'child/grandchild' syntax.

The strict syntax to address a child node is './nodeName' but you can optionally omit the './' part, which alludes to the current node, and simply use 'nodeName'.

You can also select all nodes of a given name, regardless of their location, with the syntax '//nodeName'.

The style sheet shown below matches its template to the 'sofa' node, then addresses each child of the 'sofa' node to apply formatting to them. Notice that the 'style' node uses the full form of addressing while 'size' and 'price' simply use the name of the child node:

sofas-2.xsl

```
<?xml version="1.0"?>
<xsl:stylesheet version="1.0"
    xmlns:xsl="http://www.w3.org/1999/XSL/Transform">

<xsl:template match="/">
  <html> <head> <title>Output document</title> </head>
  <body> <xsl:apply-templates/> </body> </html>
</xsl:template>

<xsl:template match="sofa">
  <big><xsl:value-of select="./style"/></big>...
  <i><xsl:value-of select="size"/></i>
  - <b>£<xsl:value-of select="price"/></b><br/>
</xsl:template>

</xsl:stylesheet>
```

This output is generated by using the style sheet on this page with the XML document on page 117.

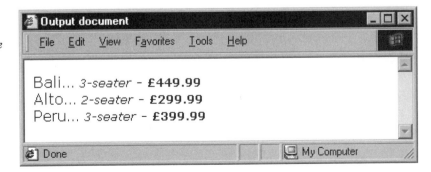

Bali... *3-seater* - **£449.99**
Alto... *2-seater* - **£299.99**
Peru... *3-seater* - **£399.99**

Addressing parent & sibling nodes

The syntax used to address the parent of the current node is '..', and siblings of the current node are addressed via their parent node using the syntax '../siblingNodeName'.

The absolute path of the 'price' node must be assigned to the 'select' attribute to prevent 'xsl:apply-templates' also generating the default output – try removing the attribute to see the difference.

For instance, if the current node, matched by the style sheet template, is the 'style' node of **sofas.xml**, '..' would address the 'sofa' node and '../price' would address the 'price' node.

The style sheet below matches the 'price' node in the style sheet template and applies formatting to its 'style' and 'size' siblings, as well as to itself as the current node. It generates output that is identical to that on the previous page but notice that with this method a 'select' attribute must be added to 'xsl:apply-templates':

sofas-3.xsl

```
<?xml version="1.0"?>
<xsl:stylesheet version="1.0"
    xmlns:xsl="http://www.w3.org/1999/XSL/Transform" >

<xsl:template match="/">
  <html> <head> <title>Output document</title> </head>
  <body>
    <xsl:apply-templates select="list/sofa/price"/>
  </body> </html>
</xsl:template>

<xsl:template match="price">
  <big><xsl:value-of select="../style"/></big>...
  <i><xsl:value-of select="../size"/></i>
  - <b>£<xsl:value-of select="."/></b><br/>
</xsl:template>
</xsl:stylesheet>
```

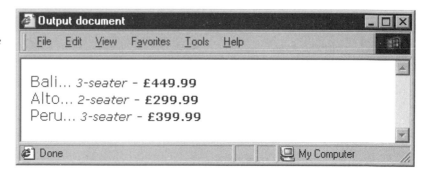

This output is generated by using the style sheet on this page with the XML document on page 117.

Output document — Bali... *3-seater* - **£449.99** / Alto... *2-seater* - **£299.99** / Peru... *3-seater* - **£399.99**

Absolute & relative addressing

It is possible to entirely ignore the current node, and relative addressing, and refer to nodes by absolute addresses instead.

Always use relative addressing unless you have a specific need to use absolute addressing – for example see page 126.

To assign an absolute address to the 'select' attribute of an 'xsl:value-of' element you must start with a '/', to denote that this address will start from root, then add the name of the root node. Add another '/', followed by the child node name as you drill down through the node tree, until you reach the required node. For instance, 'select="/list/sofa/style"'.

This is used in the style sheet below to ignore the matched 'price' node and address the 'style' node. Unfortunately, absolute addressing may not have the desired effect. Whenever the template matches a 'price' node it will apply the specified formatting to the first occurrence of the 'style' node *each time*:

sofas-4.xsl

```xml
<?xml version="1.0"?>
<xsl:stylesheet version="1.0"
    xmlns:xsl="http://www.w3.org/1999/XSL/Transform" >

<xsl:template match="/">
  <html> <head> <title>Output document</title> </head>
  <body> <xsl:apply-templates select="list/sofa/price"/>
  </body> </html>
</xsl:template>

<xsl:template match="price">
  <big><b>
    <xsl:value-of select="/list/sofa/style"/>! ...
  </b></big>
</xsl:template>
</xsl:stylesheet>
```

This output is generated by using the style sheet on this page with the XML document on page 117.

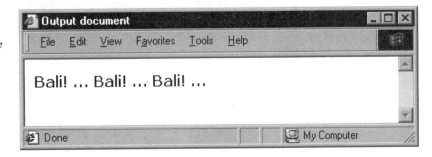

Output document window showing: Bali! ... Bali! ... Bali! ...

Addressing attribute nodes

An attribute node set can be addressed from within their containing element's node using the syntax '/@attributeName'. Any specified formatting will then be applied to each attribute in the node set when it is output.

In the following style sheet, the template matches the 'style' element, which has two attributes called 'code' and 'colour'. The generated HTML output applies formatting rules to the 'style' element itself and both of its attributes:

sofas-5.xsl

```
<?xml version="1.0"?>

<xsl:stylesheet version="1.0"
    xmlns:xsl="http://www.w3.org/1999/XSL/Transform" >

<xsl:template match="/">
  <html> <head> <title>Output document</title> </head>
  <body> <xsl:apply-templates select="list/sofa/style"/>
  </body> </html>
</xsl:template>

<xsl:template match="style">
  <!-- format each style element name -->
  The <b><xsl:value-of select="."/> </b> style has the
  <!-- format each code attribute content -->
  code number <i><xsl:value-of select="./@code"/></i>
  <!-- format each colour attribute content -->
  and is <u><xsl:value-of select="./@colour"/></u><<br/>
</xsl:template>

</xsl:stylesheet>
```

This output is generated by using the style sheet on this page with the XML document on page 117.

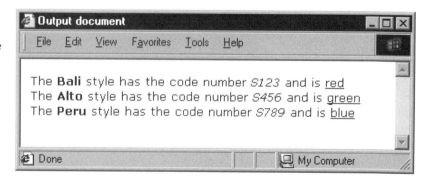

```
Output document                                    _ □ ×
 File   Edit   View   Favorites   Tools   Help

  The Bali style has the code number S123 and is red
  The Alto style has the code number S456 and is green
  The Peru style has the code number S789 and is blue

 Done                                    My Computer
```

Addressing individual elements

Elements that have unique attribute values can be singled out for selection by matching against the element and its attribute value in the template match.

Notice that the 'xsl:apply-templates' call also matches the element with the exact attribute value so that the other styles will not be output.

The style sheet below only applies formatting to the 'style' element that has a 'code' attribute value of 'S456'. So the template seeks a match for the element which has that exact attribute name and value using the syntax match= "elementName[@attributeName='attributeValue']".

Notice that the inner quotes are single whereas the outer quotes are double. This is essential with nested quotes to avoid the processor regarding the statement as being prematurely terminated:

sofas-6.xsl

```xml
<?xml version="1.0"?>
<xsl:stylesheet version="1.0"
    xmlns:xsl="http://www.w3.org/1999/XSL/Transform" >

<xsl:template match="/">
  <html> <head> <title>Output document</title> </head>
   <body> <xsl:apply-templates
              select="list/sofa/style[@code='S456']"/>
   </body> </html>
</xsl:template>

<xsl:template match="style[@code='S456']">
   The <b><xsl:value-of select="."/></b>
           style is on special offer today!
</xsl:template>

</xsl:stylesheet>
```

This output is generated by using the style sheet on this page with the XML document on page 117.

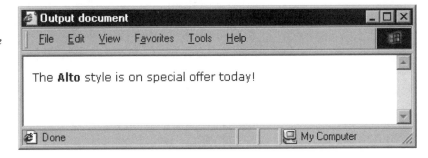

Output document

File   Edit   View   Favorites   Tools   Help

The **Alto** style is on special offer today!

Done   My Computer

Node position

A single specific node in a node set can be addressed by testing its position in the set with either the XPath 'position()' function or the 'last()' function. The first node in a set can be addressed using a 'xsl:if' test with the syntax <xsl:if test="position()=1">.

The position() function returns the position number of the current node in a set, but the last() function always returns the position number of the last node in the set. You could address the penultimate node in a set by comparing the current node's position to that of the next to last node using a 'xsl:if' test with the syntax <xsl:if test="position()=last()-1">. The style sheet below addresses two nodes individually by testing their positions:

sofas-7.xsl

```
<?xml version="1.0"?>
<xsl:stylesheet version="1.0"
    xmlns:xsl="http://www.w3.org/1999/XSL/Transform" >

<xsl:template match="/">
  <html> <head> <title>Output document</title> </head>
  <body> <xsl:apply-templates select="list/sofa/style"/>
  </body> </html>
</xsl:template>

<xsl:template match="style">
  <xsl:if test="position()=2">
    <b>Second node: <xsl:value-of select="."/></b><br/>
  </xsl:if>
  <xsl:if test="position()=last()">
    <u>Last node: <xsl:value-of select="."/></u>
  </xsl:if>
</xsl:template>
</xsl:stylesheet>
```

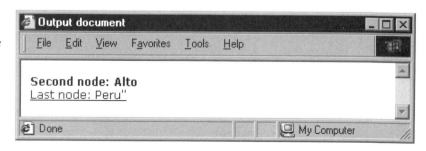

Comparing values

XPath can compare values in a test expression using any of these operators: '=' (is equal to), '!=' (is not equal to), '<' (is less than), '>' (is greater than). The entities for less and greater use the entities found in HTML to represent the '<' and '>' symbols to avoid confusion with their purpose in tags.

Additionally 'and' can be used to test if two conditions are met and 'or' can be used to provide a choice of conditions to be met.

The following style sheet uses the '<' less than operator to format sofas below £300 differently to those above that price:

sofas-8.xsl

The 'xsl:if' test is a simple conditional test that does not provide an alternative if the test fails. If you need to give that option you should use 'xsl:when' and 'xsl:otherwise' inside an 'xml:choose' block – see page 108 for an example.

```
<?xml version="1.0"?>
<xsl:stylesheet version="1.0"
    xmlns:xsl="http://www.w3.org/1999/XSL/Transform" >
<xsl:template match="/">
  <html> <head> <title>Output document</title> </head>
  <body> <xsl:apply-templates select="list/sofa/price"/>
  </body> </html>
</xsl:template>

<xsl:template match="price">
  <xsl:if test=". &lt; 300.00">
    <b>Below £300: The <xsl:value-of select="../style"/>
    sofa is just <xsl:value-of select="."/> !!!</b><br/>
  </xsl:if>
  <xsl:if test=". &gt; 300.00">
    Over £300: <xsl:value-of select="../style"/><br/>
  </xsl:if>
</xsl:template>
</xsl:stylesheet>
```

This output is generated by using the style sheet on this page with the XML document on page 117.

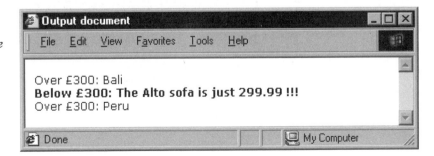

Output document

File   Edit   View   Favorites   Tools   Help

Over £300: Bali
Below £300: The Alto sofa is just 299.99 !!!
Over £300: Peru

Done   My Computer

Totalling nodes

The XPath 'count()' function returns a number that is the total of nodes in the node set specified between its brackets. This is useful to easily give a total of how many items are in a list. It may also be useful to provide a sum total of the node set values using the 'sum()' function. Like count(), the sum() function requires the node set to be specified between its brackets.

With either of these functions specify the *absolute* address of the node set so that the function can work on all its nodes.

The style sheet below outputs all the nodes, then the total number of sofas on the list and the sum total of their prices:

This example outputs the totals when the test for the last node is true –

see page 124 for more on testing node positions.

sofas-9.xsl

```xml
<?xml version="1.0"?>
<xsl:stylesheet version="1.0"
    xmlns:xsl="http://www.w3.org/1999/XSL/Transform" >
<xsl:template match="/">
  <html> <head> <title>Output document</title> </head>
  <body> <xsl:apply-templates/> </body> </html>
</xsl:template>
<xsl:template match="sofa">
  <xsl:value-of select="."/><br/>
  <xsl:if test="position()=last()">
  Total no:
  <xsl:value-of select="count(/list/sofa/price)"/><br/>
  Total price:
  <xsl:value-of select="sum(/list/sofa/price)"/>
  </xsl:if>
</xsl:template>
</xsl:stylesheet>
```

This output is generated by using the style sheet on this page with the XML document on page 117.

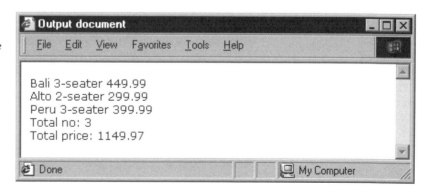

Output document

File   Edit   View   Favorites   Tools   Help

Bali 3-seater 449.99
Alto 2-seater 299.99
Peru 3-seater 399.99
Total no: 3
Total price: 1149.97

Done   My Computer

Formatting numbers

The appearance of numbers can be controlled with the XPath 'format-number()' function. This dictates a pattern to define how a number should look.

A zero in the pattern insists that the digit should always appear, even when its value is '0'. A '#' in the pattern allows zero digits to be omitted when they are insignificant to the rest of the number. Leading and trailing characters can also be added with this function.

In the following style sheet, the format-number() pattern prefixes all numbers with ':£' characters and allows any digits for thousand units to be omitted:

sofas-10.xsl

```
<?xml version="1.0"?>
<xsl:stylesheet version="1.0"
    xmlns:xsl="http://www.w3.org/1999/XSL/Transform" >

<xsl:template match="/">
  <html> <head> <title>Output document</title> </head>
  <body>
    <xsl:apply-templates/>
  </body> </html>
</xsl:template>

<xsl:template match="price">
  <xsl:value-of
      select="format-number(.,':£##,000.00')"/> <br/>
</xsl:template>

</xsl:stylesheet>
```

This output is generated by using the style sheet on this page with the XML document on page 117.

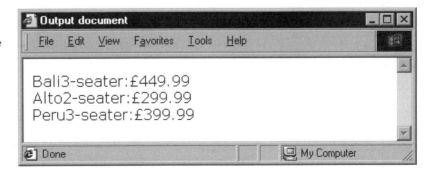

Arithmetical functions

The arithmetical operators available in XPath are listed in the table below, together with the operation that they perform:

Operator	Operation
+	Addition
-	Subtraction
*	Multiplication
div	Division
mod	Modulus

These are used in the usual way, by adding an operand before and after the operator.

A 'mod' operator returns the remainder after a division. For instance, '10 mod 2' returns 0, whereas '11 mod 2' returns 1. This can be useful to determine odd and even numbers when used in a test. So that 'if 10 mod 2=0' the number is even, otherwise it must be an odd number.

When using more than one operator in an expression it is worth noting that multiplication and division is performed before any addition and subtraction. This means that '3+6*2' is 15, not 18. Parentheses can be added to an expression to make the meaning clear, so that '(3+6)*2' *would* return 18.

The values that are actually contained in the nodes are unchanged –
XPath functions only change the generated HTML output.

All numbers are treated as double-length floating point numbers in arithmetical operations. This can lead to some lengthy fractional results when performing division. These can be formatted to display more reasonably as an integer, or with just two decimal places, using the number-format() function that is demonstrated on the previous page.

The style sheet on the facing page deducts 10% from each of the values in the 'price' nodes of the **sofas.xml** document. The arithmetic is included in a 'format-number' function to ensure that the output contains only two decimal places.

sofas-11.xsl

```
<?xml version="1.0"?>
<xsl:stylesheet version="1.0"
    xmlns:xsl="http://www.w3.org/1999/XSL/Transform" >

<xsl:template match="/">
  <html> <head> <title>Output document</title> </head>
  <body>
  <h3>Sale Prices - 10% of all items!</h3>
  <xsl:apply-templates/> </body> </html>
</xsl:template>

<xsl:template match="style">
  <!-- Add spaces -->
  <xsl:text> </xsl:text>
    <xsl:value-of select="."/>
  <xsl:text> </xsl:text>
</xsl:template>

<xsl:template match="price">
  <xsl:text> </xsl:text>
  <strike> <xsl:value-of select="."/> </strike>
  <b> Now only
  <xsl:value-of
  select="format-number(.-((.div 100)*10),'£000.00')"/>
  </b><br/>
</xsl:template>

</xsl:stylesheet>
```

Notice how the expression is bracketed to clarify the intention – 'this node minus ((this node divided by 100) multiplied by 10)'.

This output is generated by using the style sheet on this page with the XML document on page 117.

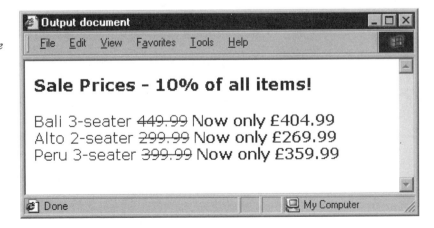

Rounding numbers

Where the number is half way between integers (.5) the round() function will round upwards.

XPath provides three functions to round floating point numbers to an integer. The 'ceiling()' function will always round up to the next integer number whereas 'floor()' will always round down to the next integer. The 'round()' function will round to the nearest integer up or down. Each function requires that the value to be rounded is specified within its brackets.

The following style sheet demonstrates both ceiling() and floor() functions to round the 'price' nodes in **sofas.xml**:

sofas-12.xsl

```
<?xml version="1.0"?>
<xsl:stylesheet version="1.0"
    xmlns:xsl="http://www.w3.org/1999/XSL/Transform" >

<xsl:template match="/">
  <html> <head> <title>Output document</title> </head>
  <body> <xsl:apply-templates select="list/sofa/price"/>
  </body> </html>
</xsl:template>

<xsl:template match="price">
  <xsl:value-of select="../style"/>: price rounded Up -
  £<xsl:value-of select="ceiling(.)"/>
  <br/><span style="background-color:silver">
  <xsl:value-of select="../style"/>: price rounded Down -
  £<xsl:value-of select="floor(.)"/> </span><br/>
</xsl:template>
</xsl:stylesheet>
```

This output is generated by using the style sheet on this page with the XML document on page 117.

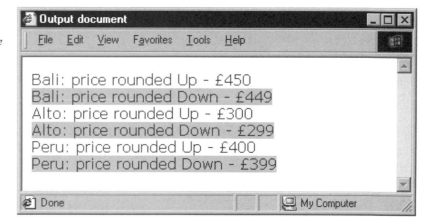

Extracting substrings

The XPath 'substring()' function allows a single character, or a piece of text, to be extracted from a string using the syntax 'substring(string, startPosition, numberOfCharacters)'.

Alternatively, 'substring-before()' and 'substring-after()' can be used to extract part of a string, starting at a specified character. Their syntax is 'substring-before/after(string, "startCharacter")'. These two functions do not have a parameter to specify the number of characters that are to be in the extracted substring.

The following style sheet extracts a single character from two existing strings to create an abbreviation for size and colour:

sofas-13.xsl

```
<?xml version="1.0"?>
<xsl:stylesheet version="1.0"
    xmlns:xsl="http://www.w3.org/1999/XSL/Transform" >
<xsl:template match="/">
  <html> <head> <title>Output document</title> </head>
  <body> <xsl:apply-templates select="list/sofa/price"/>
  </body> </html>
</xsl:template>

<xsl:template match="price">
  <xsl:value-of select="../style"/>...
  <xsl:value-of
      select="substring-before( ../size,'-' )"/>
  <xsl:value-of
      select="substring(../style/@colour,1,1)"/>
  ... £<xsl:value-of select="."/> <br/>
</xsl:template>
</xsl:stylesheet>
```

This output is generated by using the style sheet on this page with the XML document on page 117.

Output document

File   Edit   View   Favorites   Tools   Help

Bali... 3r ... £449.99
Alto... 2g ... £299.99
Peru... 3b ... £399.99

Done   My Computer

Translating text

XPath provides a function called 'translate()' which can be used to change characters in a string from uppercase to lowercase, and vice versa. This function has three parameters and uses the syntax 'translate(string, changeTheseLetters, toTheseLetters)'.

It is possible to specify individual letters to be translated but it is more common to ensure the case will be changed for all letters. This means specifying the entire alphabet, in the desired case, as the second and third parameters of the translate() function call.

The style sheet below uses the translate() function to change all strings in a 'colour' attribute to become uppercase:

sofas-14.xsl

```
<?xml version="1.0"?>
<xsl:stylesheet version="1.0"
    xmlns:xsl="http://www.w3.org/1999/XSL/Transform" >
<xsl:template match="/">
  <html> <head> <title>Output document</title> </head>
  <body> <xsl:apply-templates select="list/sofa/style"/>
  </body> </html>
</xsl:template>

<xsl:template match="style">
  <xsl:value-of select="."/> /
  <xsl:value-of select="translate(./@colour,
                        'abcdefghijklmnopqrstuvwxyz',
                        'ABCDEFGHIJKLMNOPQRSTUVWXYZ')"/> /
  <xsl:value-of select="../size"/> /
  £<xsl:value-of select="../price"/> <br/>
</xsl:template>
</xsl:stylesheet>
```

This output is generated by using the style sheet on this page with the XML document on page 117.

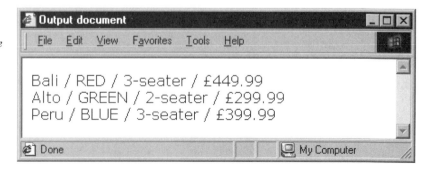

```
Output document                                    _ □ ✕
 File   Edit   View   Favorites   Tools   Help

Bali / RED / 3-seater / £449.99
Alto / GREEN / 2-seater / £299.99
Peru / BLUE / 3-seater / £399.99

Done                                    My Computer
```

Cascading StyleSheets

This chapter introduces Cascading StyleSheets (CSS) and demonstrates some CSS properties that can be used to format the content of a XML document in a variety of different ways.

Covers

Chapter Nine

What are Cascading StyleSheets?

The CSS specification was originally introduced for HTML. Over the last ten years many new tags were added to HTML, which has led to some web pages becoming very complex. CSS allows their styling controls to be separated from their page content, which makes maintenance much easier. CSS is supported by Internet Explorer and CSS style sheets work well with XML. They are ordinary plain text documents with a '**.css**' file extension.

A CSS style sheet is a list of rules which each start with a 'selector' that identifies an element of the XML document. This is followed by a pair of '{ }'curly brackets which contain 'properties' that are to be associated with the selected element.

The rule for each property states the property name, followed by a ':' colon, then a value for that property. Each property statement must be terminated with a ';' semi colon. Many CSS properties are demonstrated in this chapter to show how they format the content.

CSS is far less ambitious than XSLT and is only concerned about styling – there are no CSS functions.

A CSS style sheet is associated with a XML document using a processing instruction, in the same way that is used to associate a XSLT style sheet. In this case though, its 'type' attribute should identify the style sheet's MIME type as 'text/css'.

The simple CSS style sheet below is associated with the XML document on the opposite page. It contains a list of four property rules that are to be applied to the <make> element. When the XML document is opened in Internet Explorer the rules are applied to produce the output illustrated at the bottom of the opposite page:

vacs-1.css

```
make {    display:block;
          font-size:16pt;
          color:white;
          background-color:black;
}
```

The following XML document is used by each of the CSS examples given in this chapter. Only the style sheet file name assigned to its 'href' attribute is changed for each example. For instance, the first example assigns **vacs-1.css**, the next example assigns **vacs-2.css**, and so on.

vacs.xml

*Remember to change the value assigned to the 'href' attribute in this example, from **vacs-1.css** to the file name of the appropriate style sheet.*

```xml
<?xml version="1.0" encoding="UTF-8"?>

<!-- specify the appropriate CSS style sheet -->
<?xml:stylesheet href="vacs-1.css" type="text/css"?>

<list xsi:noNamespaceSchemaLocation="vacs.xsd"
  xmlns:xsi="http://www.w3.org/2001/XMLSchema-instance">
<vac>
  <make>Dirt Devil</make>
  <model>Ladybug</model>
  <code>405/1024</code>
  <colour>Red</colour>
  <price>39.99</price>
</vac>
<vac>
  <make>Goblin</make>
  <model>Aztec</model>
  <code>405/0018</code>
  <colour>Green</colour>
  <price>47.00</price>
</vac>
<vac>
  <make>Morphy Richards</make>
  <model>Pod</model>
  <code>405/9952</code>
  <colour>Lime/Purple</colour>
  <price>44.50</price>
</vac>
</list>
```

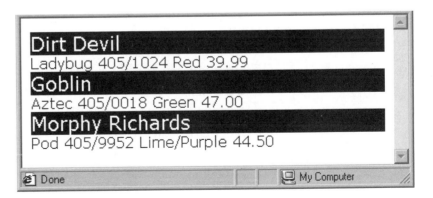

Comments & selectors

You may omit the terminating semi colon if there is just a single rule specified inside the curly brackets – the examples in this book keep them in only as a reminder that they need to be used when several rules are specified.

Single-line, or multi-line, comments may be included in a CSS style sheet between '/*' and '*/', like in the C programming language, and any comments are ignored by the browser.

A selector identifies an element of the XML document to which its rules will be applied. Several elements can be selected together by listing their names, separated by a comma, as the selector.

If two, or more, selectors point to the same element, then the rules will merge and all of them will be applied to the element. If two, or more, rules point to the same property of the same element, then the rule that appears latest (lower down) the style sheet is applied.

The commented CSS style sheet below demonstrates each of the above points in action:

vacs-2.css

```
/* Apply merged styling to just the <make> element */
make{display:block;}
make{font-family: cursive; }
make{font-size:16pt;}

/* Apply styling to both <model> and <price> elements */
model,price {font-weight:bold; }

/* Apply conflicting rules to the <code> element */
code { text-decoration:line-through; }
code { text-decoration:underline; }
```

This output is generated by using the style sheet on this page with the XML document on page 135.

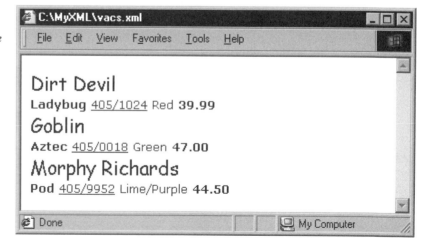

C:\MyXML\vacs.xml

File   Edit   View   Favorites   Tools   Help

Dirt Devil
Ladybug <u>405/1024</u> Red **39.99**
Goblin
Aztec <u>405/0018</u> Green **47.00**
Morphy Richards
Pod <u>405/9952</u> Lime/Purple **44.50**

Done   My Computer

Property values

There are four ways to state the value of a property in a CSS style rule: size, percentage, colour and URL. Size is expressed as a number followed immediately by one of the following units:

- px – a number of pixels

- in – a number of inches

- cm – a number of centimetres

- mm – a number of millimetres

- pt – a number of points, each point being 1/72 inch

- em – a number relative to the current font height

For instance, a font size and margin size may be set like this:

```
font-size: 12pt;
margin: 10px;
```

Percentages can be used for width, height and position and are a number immediately followed by a '%' symbol.

Shades of grey have the same proportion of red, green and blue – #222222, #555555 and #CCCCCC are all greys.

Colours can be stated as a hexadecimal value that states the proportion of red, green and blue as a value between zero (00) and 255 (FF). Therefore, #FF0000 is pure red, maximum red value but no green or blue. Similarly, #00FF00 is pure green and #0000FF is pure blue.

Alternatively, colour values can be stated using any of the keywords black, maroon, green, navy, silver, red, lime, blue, gray, purple, olive, teal, white, fuchsia, yellow or aqua. For instance, a background colour can be set to silver like this:

```
background-color: silver;
```

URLs are usually stated in CSS style sheets to specify the location of an image file with the syntax 'url(address)'. For instance, a background image can be expresses like this:

```
background: url(http://www.ineasysteps.com/logo.gif);
```

Properties & inheritance

The 'cascading' part of the CSS name refers to the way that property values are inherited by child elements of the page.

This allows whole sections of the page to be formatted with common property values very quickly. Properties of individual elements within the section can be changed with specific rules that override those for the general section.

The style sheet below illustrates this by setting four rules that apply to the <vac> element. These cascade down to also apply to all its child elements. Specific rules are then added to the style sheet to change individual properties of just two of those child elements:

vacs-3.css

```
/* Apply styling to the <vac> parent element which
   will cascade down to all its child elements */

vac {      display:block;
           font-family: cursive;
           font-size:16pt;
           color:black;
}

/* Apply special styling to change the colour of the
   <code> and <price> elements only */

code {     color:silver;}

price{     text-decoration:underline; }
```

This output is generated by using the style sheet on this page with the XML document on page 135.

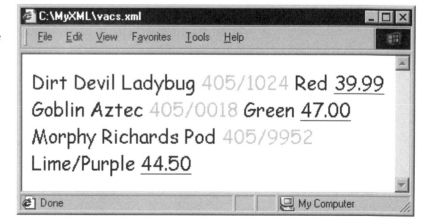

C:\MyXML\vacs.xml

File   Edit   View   Favorites   Tools   Help

Dirt Devil Ladybug 405/1024 Red 39.99
Goblin Aztec 405/0018 Green 47.00
Morphy Richards Pod 405/9952
Lime/Purple 44.50

Done   My Computer

The content box

The browser displays each element of the page in an invisible box that has several properties which can be adjusted by a CSS style sheet. This may be a 'block' box, that has a line break before and after it, or an 'inline' box that appears on a single line within a block box. This illustration identifies the properties of the content box:

Block boxes are most important for arranging the layout of a document's contents on the screen.

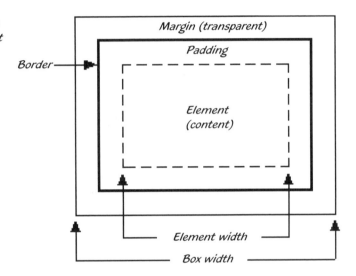

The padding property defines the edges of the content box. With a padding width of zero the content box edges are identical to the contained content edges. The content box edges extend as the padding width is increased.

The border property defines the width of the area immediately surrounding the content box. With a border width of zero the border edges remain identical to the content box edges. The border edges extend as the border width is increased.

The margin property defines the width of the area that immediately surrounds the border edges. With a margin width of zero the margin edges remain identical to the border edges. The margin edges extend as the margin width is increased.

A style rule can specify the value for all four sides of a property or individual sides can be addressed with the top, bottom, left and right part of each property.

Border styles

The style of all four borders around a content box can be set collectively with a 'border-style' property.

Alternatively, the style of each side of a border can be specified individually using 'border-style-top', 'border-style-bottom', 'border-style-left' and 'border-style-right'.

The available border styles are illustrated below, together with the name that can be specified as the value of any border property:

 To apply a border style a width and colour must also be specified – see the example on the facing page.

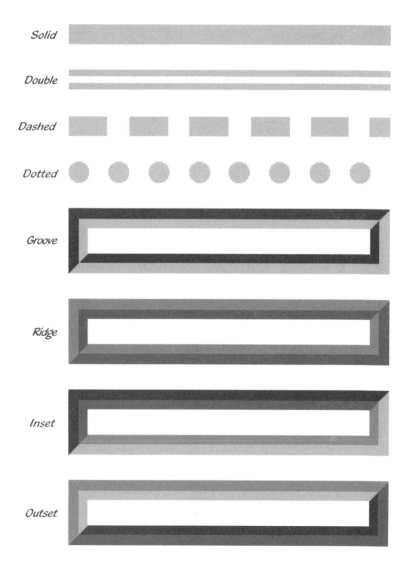

Solid

Double

Dashed

Dotted

Groove

Ridge

Inset

Outset

...cont'd

See overleaf for examples that add padding and margin space.

The CSS style sheet below adds a dashed border around all the block boxes of each <make> element. It also adds a solid border around all the inline boxes of the other elements.

Notice that the block box borders occupy the full width of the page but the inline box borders just surround the content. Also note the default padding space, between the content and the border, and see how the boxes sit directly below each other because the default top and bottom margin space around the boxes is set at zero:

vacs-4.css

```
/* set general rules*/
vac{        display:inline;
            font-family: cursive;
            font-size:12pt;
            color:black;

}

/* Apply styling to the <make> element */
make {      display:block;
            font-size:16pt;
            border: 5px dashed black;

}

/* Apply border styling to all other elements */
model,code,colour,price {border: 1px solid black; }
```

This output is generated by using the style sheet on this page with the XML document on page 135.

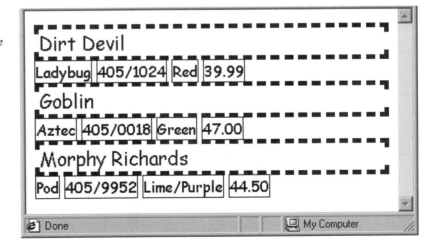

Setting margins

A uniform margin can be specified in a CSS style rule with the 'margin' property, or individual margins can be set using 'margin-top', 'margin-bottom', 'margin-left' or 'margin-right'.

Alternatively, different margins can be set around a content box by specifying multiple sizes to the margin property, using this syntax:

```
margin: topMargin,rightMargin,bottomMargin,leftMargin;
```

Margin values can be stated as percentages, or as absolute lengths like in the style sheet below that sets uniform margins of 10 pixels:

vacs-5.css

```
vac{      display:inline; color:black;
          font-family: cursive; font-size:12pt;
}
make{     display:block; font-size:16pt;
          border: 1px solid black; margin:10px;
}
model,code,colour,price{
          border: 1px solid black; margin:10px;
}
```

This output is generated by using the style sheet on this page with the XML document on page 135.

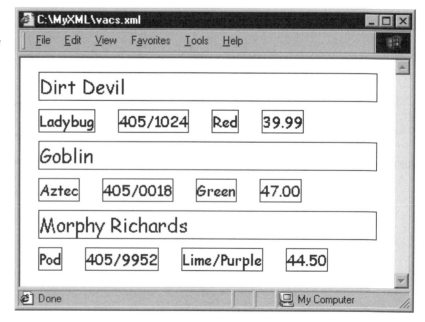

Adding padding

A uniform padding value can be specified in a CSS style rule with the 'padding' property, or individual padding can be set using 'padding-top', 'padding-bottom', 'padding-left' or 'padding-right'.

Alternatively, various padding can be set around a box's content by specifying multiple values to the padding property like this:

```
padding: topPad, rightPad, bottomPad, leftPad;
```

Padding values can be stated as percentages, or as absolute lengths like in the style sheet below that sets uniform padding of 1mm:

vacs-6.css

```
vac{        display:inline; color:black;
            font-family: cursive; font-size:12pt; }

make{       display:block; font-size:16pt; margin:10px;
            border: 1px solid black; padding:1mm; }

model,code,colour,price{ border: 1px solid black;
            margin:10px; padding:1mm; }
```

This output is generated by using the style sheet on this page with the XML document on page 135.

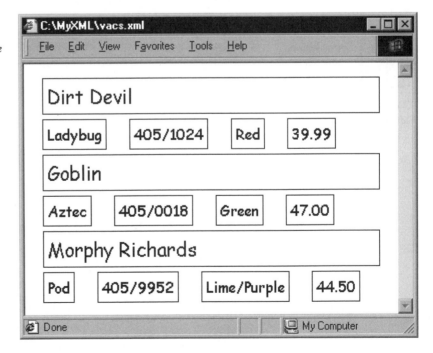

Positioning boxes

The position of a content box can be adjusted, from that of the normal flow layout of other boxes, using a style rule with the 'position' property set to 'relative'. Then, a 'left' property can be assigned a length value to shift the box's position horizontally. Additionally, a 'top' property can specify a length value to adjust the box's position vertically.

The style sheet below insets the position of all boxes except those containing <make> elements. The amount of adjustment could have been specified as an absolute length but in this example it is set to shift the position by 5% to the right:

vacs-7.css

```
vac{      display:inline; color:black;
          font-family: cursive; font-size:12pt; }

make{     display:block; font-size:16pt; margin:10px;
          border: 1px solid black;  padding:1mm; }

model,code,colour,price{ border: 1px solid black;
          margin:10px; padding:1mm;
          position:relative; left: +5%; }
```

This output is generated by using the style sheet on this page with the XML document on page 135.

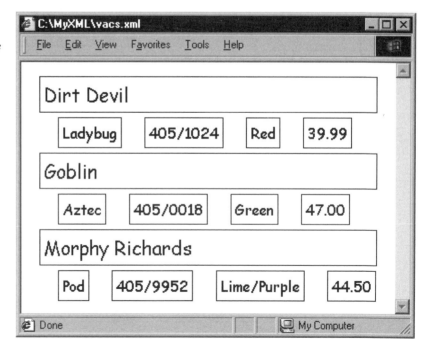

Text alignment & decoration

Text within a content box is left-aligned by default but this can be changed by adding a style rule with a 'text-align' property. Possible values that can be assigned are 'left', 'right' or 'center'.

Lines can be added to the text in a content box by a style rule using a 'text-decoration' property. This can add an 'underline', an 'overline', or a 'line-through', to the text.

The style sheet below centres the text within the <make> element's content boxes and adds an example of each type of text-decoration line in some of the other element's boxes:

vacs-8.css

```
vac{        display:inline; color:black;
            font-family: cursive; font-size:12pt; }

make {      display:block;  font-size:16pt; padding:1mm;
            margin:5px; border:1px solid black;
            text-align:center; }

price { text-decoration:underline; }
code { text-decoration:overline; }
colour { text-decoration:line-through; }
```

This output is generated by using the style sheet on this page with the XML document on page 135.

Setting fonts

Every aspect of the font, that is used by the browser to display text content, can be specified in CSS style rules.

The font can be made italic by adding a 'font-style' property rule with its value set to 'italic'. It can also be made bold by adding a 'font-weight' property rule with a value of 'bold'. Adding both of these rules to a single element will display its text in a font that is both bold and italic.

The size of the font to be used can be specified as a point value to the 'font-size' property. A medium size font is around 10 points high so a rule to set this size could look like this:

```
elementName: { font-size: 10pt; }
```

The 'font-family' property can specify the name of the font that is to be used to display an element's text content. It is advisable to list several font names in case the preferred font is not available to the browser. A generic family name can also be used to set a font as either 'serif', 'sans-serif', 'cursive', 'fantasy', or 'monospace'.

In the example below , the font-family property rule first attempts to set a serif font called Garamond. If that is unavailable locally the rule attempts to set the Times New Roman serif font. If that too is unavailable the rule asks the browser to use its default serif font:

```
font-family: { "Garamond", "Times New Roman", serif; }
```

The fonts below are typically used as the generic default fonts:

serif

sans-serif

cursive

fANTASY

monospace

A style rule can specify several font values at once using the 'font' property. This amalgamates all of the font properties on the opposite page into a single rule with this syntax:

```
font: font-style font-weight font-size font-family;
```

The following CSS style sheet uses the font property to assign various font values for each of the elements in the XML document:

vacs-9.css

```
/* set font: style weight size family */

make{
    display:block; font: normal normal 26pt fantasy; }

model {
    display:inline; font: italic normal 14pt sans-serif; }

price {
    display:inline; font: normal bold 14pt cursive; }

code {
    display:inline;  font: normal normal 14pt serif ; }

colour {
    display:inline;  font: normal normal 14pt monospace; }
```

This output is generated by using the style sheet on this page with the XML document on page 135.

Letter spacing

Extra space can be added between each character of the text in a content box with a CSS style rule 'letter-spacing' property.

Use 'em' units in preference to pixels to display the text in spacing that is appropriate to the text size.

This property can specify a length to be added to the default text spacing between characters.

The extra space may be a distance expressed as pixels, like '10px'.

Alternatively, the extra space can be expressed as a distance relative to the font size by using an 'em' unit like '1em'.

The style sheet below displays all text content in monospace font but adds 16 pixels between the letters of the <make> element:

vacs-10.css

```
/* default styles */

vac {
        display:inline;
        font-family:monospace;
}

/* set make element styles */]

make{
        display:block;
        text-decoration:underline;
        letter-spacing:16px;
}
```

This output is generated by using the style sheet on this page with the XML document on page 135.

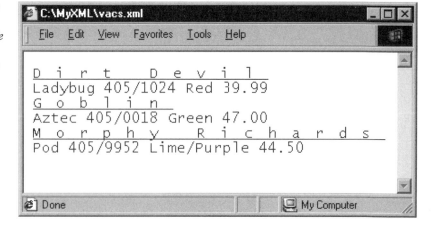

Capitalising text

The 'text-transform' property can be used in CSS style rules to convert the capitalisation of text content.

Text may not be transformed for content in languages that use other than standard Latin characters.

It may be used to transform the text into 'uppercase', or 'lowercase', or it may be used to make the first letter of each word into a capital letter when its value is set to 'capitalize'.

The style sheet below uses the text-transform property to make the text content of each <make> element into uppercase, and the text content of each <colour> element into lowercase:

vacs-11.css

```
/* set default styles */

vac{      display:inline;
          font: 14pt serif;
}

/* set make element styles */

make {    display:block;
          font-weight:bold;
          text-transform:uppercase;
}

/* set color element styles */

colour { text-transform:lowercase;
}
```

This output is generated by using the style sheet on this page with the XML document on page 135.

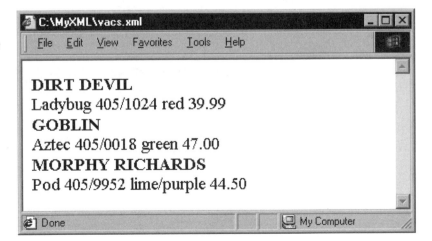

```
C:\MyXML\vacs.xml
File   Edit   View   Favorites   Tools   Help

DIRT DEVIL
Ladybug 405/1024 red 39.99
GOBLIN
Aztec 405/0018 green 47.00
MORPHY RICHARDS
Pod 405/9952 lime/purple 44.50

Done                                    My Computer
```

Content visibility

A style sheet can prevent the content of an element being displayed on the page in two different ways. A style rule can set its 'display' property to 'none' so that no content box for that element is shown on the page. Alternatively, a style rule can set the elements 'visibility' property to 'hide' which will include its content box on the page but will not show its contents.

This style sheet does not display any <code> elements:

```
vac { display:block; font: 12pt sans-serif; }
code {display:none; }
```

vacs-12.css

This output is generated by using the style sheet on this page with the XML document on page 135.

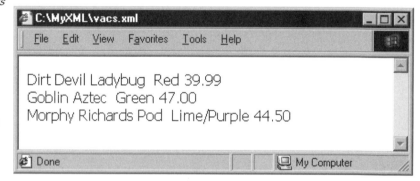

This style sheet includes space for the content boxes of the <code> elements but does not actually display their content:

```
vac { display:block; font: 14pt sans-serif; }
code {visibility:hidden; }
```

vacs-13.css

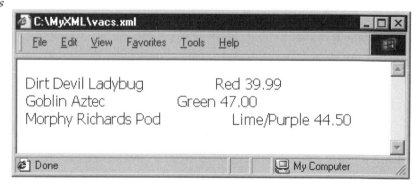

Foreground & background colours

A style rule can specify the text colour for an element by setting a value for its 'color' property. Similarly, the background colour of an element can be specified in a style rule that sets a value for its 'background-color' property.

See page 137 for details about valid colour values.

The desired colour can be specified as a hexadecimal value, like #FF0000 for red, #000000 for white, or #0000FF for blue, or as one of the recognised colour keywords, such as 'red', 'white' or 'blue'.

The style sheet below sets both foreground and background colours for the <make> element and a common background for all other elements:

vacs-14.css

```
/* set default styles */
vac {
        display:block;
        font: bold 16pt serif;
        background-color:silver; }

/* set make element styles */
make {
        display:block;
        color:#FFFFFF;
        background-color:gray; }
```

This output is generated by using the style sheet on this page with the XML document on page 135.

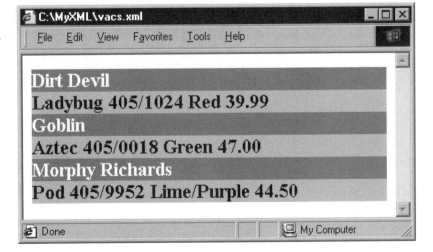

Background image

As an alternative to setting a background colour for an element, an image may be specified using the 'background-image' property in a style rule.

This must state the image's location using this syntax:

```
background-image: url ( fileName );
```

It is usually appropriate to set the height of the content box to match the height of the image by adding a 'height' style rule.

The style sheet below adds a background image of 44 pixels high to the <make> element. Notice that the image tiles repeatedly across the background of the <make> element's content boxes:

vacs-15.css

sun.gif

```
vac {      display:block;
           background-color:silver; }

make{      display:block;
           font: bold 32pt serif;
           height:44px;
           background-image: url("sun.gif"); }
```

This output is generated by using the style sheet on this page with the XML document on page 135.

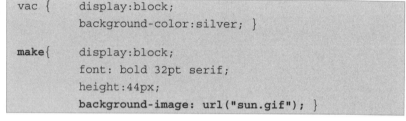

Background position

The position of a background image in a content box can be controlled by adding a 'background-position' style rule. Possible values for this property can be expressed as two absolute lengths from the left and top edges of the content box, or with two descriptive keywords 'top', 'bottom', 'left' or 'right'.

A background image can be prevented from tiling repeatedly across the content box by adding a style rule that sets a 'background-repeat' property to 'no-repeat'. This will allow the background image to appear just once.

The style sheet below adds a single image to each <make> element and uses a 'text-indent' property to indent their text content in order to fully reveal the images:

vacs-16.css

flash.gif

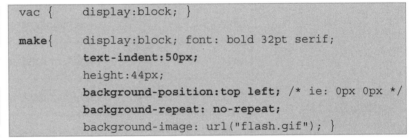

```
vac {        display:block; }

make{        display:block; font: bold 32pt serif;
             text-indent:50px;
             height:44px;
             background-position:top left; /* ie: 0px 0px */
             background-repeat: no-repeat;
             background-image: url("flash.gif"); }
```

This output is generated by using the style sheet on this page with the XML document on page 135.

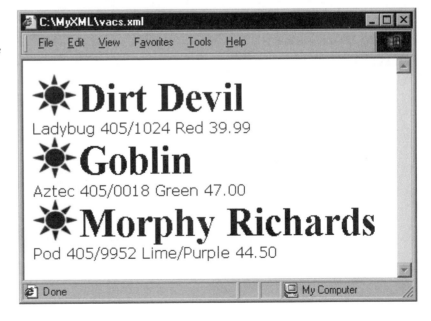

Cursors

The type of cursor to be displayed over elements can be specified with the CSS style 'cursor' property.

Common valid cursor values include 'default', 'crosshair', 'move', 'text', 'wait', and 'help', as seen in the table below:

The browser will determine the precise appearance of each cursor.

Name	Cursor	Pointer Type
default		Browser's default cursor
crosshair		Pinpoint selector
move		Selection relocator
text		Text highlighter
wait		Program busy indicator
help		Help available indicator
resize		Edge indicator
url		Specify remote cursor address
hand		Hyperlink indicator

The hand cursor is used in the example on page 161.

The resize cursor is a pointer that indicates a direction and can be set as 'n-resize', 's-resize', 'w-resize', 'e-resize', 'ne-resize', 'nw-resize', 'se-resize', or 'sw-resize'. In the table above the 'e-resize' cursor is illustrated.

A custom cursor can be used by specifying the location of a cursor image with the term 'url', such as this example:

```
cursor: url( "http://domain/folder/special.cur" );
```

The location is stated as either a relative or absolute address between quotes and inside brackets after the 'url' term.

XLink and XPointer

This chapter introduces the XML Linking Language (XLink) and the XML Pointer Language (XPointer) which are designed to create links between files. At the time of writing, both language specifications are complete but are not currently supported by Internet Explorer. The examples illustrated in this chapter speculate on how XML linking may work.

Covers

Chapter Ten

Simple links

The XLink language allows links between documents to be expressed in XML. A 'simple' link is similar to a HTML link, that is written with an <A> anchor tag, and links to a single document.

Simple links are elements of the XLink namespace which define the link by assigning values to the element's attributes. The XML code below creates a link in a XLink element called 'xlink:simple':

The XLink namespace could alternatively have been declared in the root element – to become available to the entire document.

```
<xlink:simple
        xmlns:xlink="http://www.w3.org/1999/xlink"
        xlink:href="http://www.ineasysteps.com"
        xlink:role="booklist"
        xlink:title="Visit the EASY STEPS home page"
        xlink:show="replace"
        xlink:actuate="onRequest">
Click here to explore the full range of EASY STEPS books
</xlink:simple>
```

The purpose of each attribute in a simple link is as follows:

- 'xmlns:xlink' declares the standard XLink namespace that is always the URL **http://www.w3.org/1999/xlink**

- 'xlink:href' states the URL of the target document

- 'xlink:role' assigns a descriptive name to the link that can be read by other machines to identify the link

- 'xlink:title' assigns a description of the link that can be read by the user, like a tooltip in a HTML link

- 'xlink:show' determines where the target document should appear. Assigning a 'replace' value will replace the current document with the target document, like a standard HTML link. An 'embedded' value will include the target document in the current page and a 'new' value will display the target document in a new window

- 'xlink:actuate' determines when the link will call the target document. A value of 'onRequest' requires a user action, like a mouse click, to activate the link. A value of 'onLoad' will activate the link when the document loads into the browser.

An existing XML element can be made into a link by including all the XLink attributes inside the element's opening tag together with a 'xlink:type' attribute. This must be assigned a 'simple' value to declare the element to be a simple link.

For instance, the link in the previous example could be rewritten as an element called 'simpleLink' like this:

```
<simpleLink
        xlink:type="simple"
        xmlns:xlink="http://www.w3.org/1999/xlink"
        xlink:href="http://www.ineasysteps.com"
        xlink:role="booklist"
        xlink:title="Visit the EASY STEPS home page"
        xlink:show="replace"
        xlink:actuate="onRequest">
Click here to explore the full range of EASY STEPS books
</simpleLink>
```

XLink is another example of how XML technologies can offer more power than previous ones, in the same way that XSLT style sheets are more powerful than CSS style sheets.

Both previous examples create a link that is similar to a HTML hyperlink, where the user clicks on the link text to replace the current document in the browser with a target document.

It is important to note, though, that XLink can be used to link any type of resource to the XML document and adds greater flexibility to the way in which those resources may be used.

The code below defines a link which embeds an image into the page when the browser opens the XML document:

The <picture> element in this example is an empty element.

```
<picture
        xlink:type="simple"
        xmlns:xlink="http://www.w3.org/1999/xlink"
        xlink:href="jacket.jpg"
        xlink:role="showCover"
        xlink:title="See the book cover"
        xlink:show="embedded"
        xlink:actuate="onLoad"/>
```

Extended links

A XPath extended link simultaneously connects multiple documents, or other resources, to a XML document.

The structure of an extended link has a fundamental element, with a XLink namespace declaration and a 'xlink:type' attribute set to 'extended'. A description of the link is assigned to a 'xlink:role' attribute and its name is assigned to a 'xlink:title' attribute.

The tags of this element surround other elements containing information about the linked files, and optionally how they may be traversed. This entire set of link elements, including the fundamental element, is collectively known as a 'linkset'.

The code below illustrates the structure of a linkset that has a fundamental element called 'extendedLink':

```
<extendedLink
        xmlns:xlink="http://www.w3.org/1999/xlink"
        xlink:type="extended"
        xlink:role="moreBooks"
        xlink:title="More EASY STEPS titles" >

    ( descriptions of the link files are added here )

    ( optional traversing definitions are added here )

</extendedLink>
```

Descriptions of files to be linked to the XML document are added first inside the linkset. Each of these elements describes the link by specifying values to its various XLink attributes.

If the link is to an external file the element's 'xlist:type' attribute should be assigned a value of 'locator'. If the link is to a point within the original document, like a HTML fragment identifier, the element's 'xlist:type' attribute should be assigned a value of 'resource'.

The actual address of the link's location is assigned to a 'xlink:href' attribute, then descriptive names are assigned to a 'xlink:role' attribute and a 'xlink:title' attribute.

The code below could be added to the previous example to become the link descriptions of the extendedLink linkset:

```
<src xlink:type="locator"
    xlink:href="Perl-book.xml" xlink:role="perlBook"
    xlink:title="CGI &amp; Perl in easy steps" />

<src xlink:type="locator"
    xlink:href="Java-book.xml" xlink:role="javaBook"
    xlink:title="Java 2 in easy steps" />

<src xlink:type="locator"
    xlink:href="WAP-book.xml" xlink:role="wapBook"
    xlink:title="WAP in easy steps" />
```

The Wireless Application Protocol (WAP) is a XML application.

The optional traversing definitions for the link files are added to the linkset using the 'xlink:arc' attribute. These elements assign the starting point of a link to their 'xlink:from' attribute and the destination point of the link to their 'xlink:to' attribute. The value of the 'xlink:role' attributes in the locator elements are used to identify each point.

A 'xlink:actuate' attribute will determine when the link is to be activated by assigning values of 'onLoad' or 'onRequest'. Also the element's 'xlink:show' attribute can determine where the link will be displayed with values of 'replace', 'embedded' or 'new'.

This example describes three links in the <extendedLink> element then defines the order in which they may be traversed.
The code in this example could be added to the previous examples to become the connection definitions of the extendedLink linkset.

```
<go xlink:type="arc"
    xlink:from="perlBook" xlink:to="javaBook"
    xlink:show="replace"
    xlink:actuate="onRequest" />

<go xlink:type="arc"
    xlink:from="javaBook" xlink:to="wapBook"
    xlink:show="replace"
    xlink:actuate="onRequest" />

<go xlink:type="arc"
    xlink:from="wapBook" xlink:to="perlBook"
    xlink:show="replace"
    xlink:actuate="onRequest" />
```

Displaying simple & extended links

As XLink is not currently supported by Internet Explorer it is impossible to know how its features will be used by the browser but the following example suggests how it may work:

link.xml

The XML document on the right includes both a simple link and an extended link. Note the following:

- *when the user selects the simple link a new window opens to display the target file*

- *when the user selects the extended link a window opens to present a menu of possible links to the user taking their role value to represent each menu item*

```xml
<?xml version="1.0" encoding="UTF-8"?>
<?xml:stylesheet href="link.css" type="text/css"?>
<root>
<para>
The Porsche 911 is the most practical of all supercars.
<br/>Click
    <simpleLink
      xlink:type="simple"
      xmlns:xlink="http://www.w3.org/1999/xlink"
      xlink:href="porsche911.jpg" xlink:role="image"
      xlink:title="See a picture of this car"
      xlink:show="new" xlink:actuate="onRequest"> here
    </simpleLink>
to see a picture of this fabulous sports car.
</para>
<para>
For a menu of other supercar marques click
    <extendedLink
        xlink:type="extended"
        xmlns:xlink="http://www.w3.org/1999/xlink"
        xlink:role="show menu"
        xlink:title="Supercars menu ">
<src xlink:type="locator" xlink:href="diablo.jpg"
                    xlink:role="Lamborghini Diablo"/>
<src xlink:type="locator" xlink:href="mclarenf1.jpg"
                    xlink:role="Mclaren F1"/>
<src xlink:type="locator" xlink:href="ferrari355.jpg"
                    xlink:role="Ferrari 355"/> here
        </extendedLink>
    </para>
</root>
```

...cont'd

This illustration is just an interpretation of how Internet Explorer might display multiple link options.

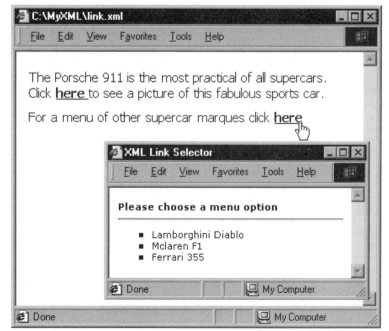

Linking by element identity

The XPointer language is used to recognise specific elements in a XML document. This is useful to create links to particular elements, like fragment identifiers in HTML, when used in conjunction with XLink.

XPointer can search the elements of a XML document to seek any which have an 'id' attribute. Their value is compared against that specified to XPointer in order to attempt a match. When a unique match has been found, XPointer has identified that specific element so it can become the target of an individual link.

The XML document below contains a simple link to the element with an id attribute value of 'gold' in the bottom XML document:

shower-1.xml

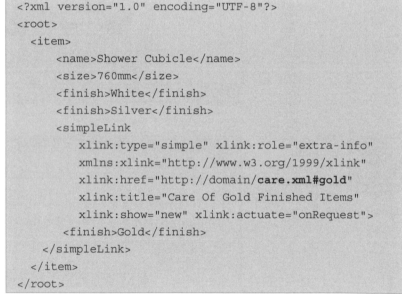

```
<?xml version="1.0" encoding="UTF-8"?>
<root>
   <item>
      <name>Shower Cubicle</name>
      <size>760mm</size>
      <finish>White</finish>
      <finish>Silver</finish>
      <simpleLink
         xlink:type="simple" xlink:role="extra-info"
         xmlns:xlink="http://www.w3.org/1999/xlink"
         xlink:href="http://domain/care.xml#gold"
         xlink:title="Care Of Gold Finished Items"
         xlink:show="new" xlink:actuate="onRequest">
      <finish>Gold</finish>
   </simpleLink>
   </item>
</root>
```

All examples in this chapter are based upon the specifications but are unable to be tested in a browser.

care.xml

```
<?xml version="1.0" encoding="UTF-8"?>
<root>
   <heading>Care of Shower Cubicle Frames</heading>
   <frame id="white">Wash with soap and water</frame>
   <frame id="silver">May be highly polished</frame>
   <frame id="gold">Wash with soap and water. Special
      care must be taken to protect this finish - never
      use abrasives or solutions when cleaning.</frame>
</root>
```

Linking by element position

Omit the URL if you want XPointer to point to an element in the same document.

XPointer can be used to link to a specific element within a XML document by identifying it with a XPath expression.

The syntax to identify the element looks like this:

```
url # xpointer( elementName [ xpathExpression ] )
```

In the example below a simple link is created. XPointer uses a XPath position() function to identify the first element named 'frame' in the XML document at the bottom of the page:

shower-2.xml

```
<?xml version="1.0" encoding="UTF-8"?>
<root>
   <item>
       <name>Shower Cubicle</name>
       <size>760mm</size>
       <simpleLink
           xlink:type="simple"
           xlink:role="extra-info"
           xmlns:xlink="http://www.w3.org/1999/xlink"
     xlink:href=
     "http://domain/care.xml#xpointer(frame[position()=1])"
           xlink:title="Care Of White Finished Items"
           xlink:show="new" xlink:actuate="onRequest">
         <finish>White</finish>
       </simpleLink>
       <finish>Silver</finish>
       <finish>Gold</finish>
     </item>
</root>
```

care.xml

```
<?xml version="1.0" encoding="UTF-8"?>
<root>
   <heading>Care of Shower Cubicle Frames</heading>
   <frame id="white">Wash with soap and water</frame>
   <frame id="silver">May be highly polished</frame>
   <frame id="gold">Wash with soap and water. Special
     care must be taken to protect this finish - never
     use abrasives or solutions when cleaning.</frame>
</root>
```

Linking by element hierarchy

XPointer can be used to link to a specific element within a XML document by identifying it with a 'child sequence' that defines its position in the document hierarchy.

The child sequence begins with a '/' forward slash character to denote the root element. This is followed by a number denoting the position of a child of the root element. For instance the fifth child of a root element would have the child sequence '/5'.

The example below creates a link to the third child of the root element in the XML document at the bottom of the page:

shower-3.xml

A child sequence can also represent other descendants of the root element – the 2nd grandchild of the 3rd child element would be '/3/2'.

```
<?xml version="1.0" encoding="UTF-8"?>
<root>
    <item>
        <name>Shower Cubicle</name>
        <size>760mm</size>
        <simpleLink
            xlink:type="simple"
            xlink:role="extra-info"
            xmlns:xlink="http://www.w3.org/1999/xlink"
            xlink:href="http://domain/care.xml#/3"
            xlink:title="Care Of Silver Finished Items"
            xlink:show="new"
            xlink:actuate="onRequest">
          <finish>White</finish>
        </simpleLink>
        <finish>Silver</finish>
        <finish>Gold</finish>
    </item>
</root>
```

care.xml

```
<?xml version="1.0" encoding="UTF-8"?>
<root>
    <heading>Care of Shower Cubicle Frames</heading>
    <frame id="white">Wash with soap and water</frame>
    <frame id="silver">May be highly polished</frame>
    <frame id="gold">Wash with soap and water. Special
        care must be taken to protect this finish - never
        use abrasives or solutions when cleaning.</frame>
</root>
```

XML DOM

This chapter introduces the XML Document Object Model (DOM) and explains some of its properties and methods. A working application demonstrates how a XML document can be embedded in a HTML page to provide an inbuilt database. JavaScript is used to extract specific pieces of data and dynamically display them in the browser.

Covers

Chapter Eleven

What is the XML DOM?

The XML DOM is a programming interface that provides a way for properties of a document to be accessed and manipulated. Using the DOM, a programmer can navigate a document's structure, and add, modify, or delete its elements.

One important objective for the DOM is to provide a standard programming interface that can be used with any programming language. The Microsoft XML parser supports JavaScript, VBScript, Perl, VB, Java, C++ and other programming languages.

DOM represents each node of a document's node tree as an object, starting from the top level which is the 'Document' object, and working down through each of the document's child node levels.

A top level XML Document object, called in this case 'xmlDoc', can be created in a HTML document using this JavaScript code:

The examples in this chapter will feature only JavaScript code, as that is the more common language.

```
var xmlDoc = new ActiveXObject("Microsoft.XMLDOM")
```

VBScript can create a XML Document object with this code:

```
set xmlDoc = CreateObject("Microsoft.XMLDOM")
```

Once the Document object has been created, an existing XML document can be loaded into it. The code below loads a XML document called **simple.xml** into the 'xmlDoc' Document object:

```
<script type="text/javascript">

var xmlDoc = new ActiveXObject("Microsoft.XMLDOM");
xmlDoc.async="false";
xmlDoc.load("simple.xml");

// ...code to process the document is added here

</script>
```

The first line of the script above creates a Document object and the second line ensures that the XML parser will halt execution until the document is fully loaded. The third line tells the parser to load a XML document called **simple.xml**.

DOM nodes

Each aspect of a XML document is represented as an individual node in the XML DOM. There are, however, several different types of node according to what they represent. These are listed in the table below together with each identifying code number that is stored in a DOM property called 'nodeType':

A script can identify each type of node by making a conditional test against their code numbers, e.g. 'if (node.nodeType==1)' could seek element nodes.

Code	Node Type	Example
1	Element	<element>
2	Attribute	name="value"
3	Text	This is some text content.
4	CDATA section	<![CDATA[characters]]>
5	Entity reference	©
6	Entity	<!ENTITY copy "#169;">
7	Processing instruction	<?xml:stylesheet >
8	Comment	<!-- comment here -->
9	Document	<root>
10	Document type	<!DOCTYPE>
11	Document fragment	url#fragment
12	Notation	<!NOTATION>

The DOM property 'nodeName' stores the name of the node. For instance, with an element nodeType this is the name of that tag.

Another DOM property called 'nodeValue' stores the value of the node. For a text nodeType this is the actual text.

Addressing XML elements

The topmost element in the node tree of a XML document is represented in the DOM by the 'documentElement' property of the Document object. This will be the root element of the XML document and has the syntax 'Document.documentElement'.

XML data embedded in a HTML document is referred to as a 'XML Data Island'.

It is useful to determine if the documentElement contains any child elements by interrogating its 'hasChildNodes' property. This returns true if child elements are found, otherwise it returns false.

Children of documentElement are represented by its 'childNodes' property. The sum total number of child elements is stored in the 'length' property of childNodes, that has the full syntax of 'Document.documentElement.childNodes.length'.

Knowing the total number of child elements is useful in creating a loop to examine each child element with the 'item()' method of the childNodes property. This method takes an integer argument to identify the position of an element, for instance 'item(0)' is the first child element. The loop can start at zero for the first child and continue to the last child when the childNodes.length limit is met.

The following example writes out the documentElement root tag name followed by the sum total of its child elements. A loop function then lists the names of all the child tag names using the 'nodeName' property of each node. The XML document that is loaded by the JavaScript in this example is shown below:

simple.xml

```
<?xml version="1.0"?>
<cameras>
    <make>Kodak</make>
    <model code="561/8019">Easyshare DX3600</model>
    <price>349.00</price>

    <make>Nikon</make>
    <model code="561/7687">Coolpix 880</model>
    <price>549.00</price>

    <make>Fujifilm</make>
    <model code="561/8150">Finepix 6800</model>
    <price>649.99</price>

</cameras>
```

The JavaScript is contained in the HTML document shown below and the output is illustrated at the bottom of this page:

simple.html

```
<html> <head> <title>XML Data Island</title>
<script type="text/javascript">
var xmlDoc=new ActiveXObject("Microsoft.XMLDOM");
xmlDoc.async="false";
xmlDoc.load("simple.xml");
document.write("The root element tag is called ");
document.write(xmlDoc.documentElement.nodeName);

if(xmlDoc.documentElement.hasChildNodes)
{
document.write("<br/>It contains ");
document.write(xmlDoc.documentElement.childNodes.length);
document.write(" child elements called...");
for(var i=0;
    i < xmlDoc.documentElement.childNodes.length; i++)
  {
    document.write("<br/>"+
    xmlDoc.documentElement.childNodes.item(i).nodeName);
  }
}
else document.write("It contains no child elements");
</script>
</head> <body> </body> </html>
```

The syntax for the XML DOM can become unwieldy – it's common to use variables to shorten the code. For instance 'var root = xmlDoc.documentElement' so that the code testing for child elements becomes 'if(root.hasChildNodes)'.

```
The root element tag is called cameras
It contains 9 child elements called...
make
model
price
make
model
price
make
model
price
```

Done   My Computer

Getting element contents

The argument name must be enclosed in quotes.

The XML DOM Document object has a method called getElementsByTagName() that can be used to address all the elements of a XML document bearing the name specified as the method's argument between its parentheses. For instance, you can use 'Document.getElementsByTagName("name")' to address all elements called <name> in a XML document. This method matches all those named elements in the order in which they appear in the document.

getElementsByTagName() has a sub-method called item() that can be used to address an individual item within the matched elements. This takes an integer as its argument to identify an element's position in the matched sequence, For instance, to address the first occurrence of an element called <name> you would use the code 'Document.getElementsByTagName("name").item(0)'.

The item() method has a property called 'text' that retrieves the text content of the element it addresses. So to get the text content of the first occurrence of a <name> element would require the code 'Document.getElementsByTagName("name").item(0).text'.

getElementsByTagName() also has a 'length' property that stores the sum total number of elements matching the specified element name. This is useful to set a maximum limit for a loop through those elements.

The following example addresses all occurrences of an element called <make> in the **simple.xml** document, shown on page 168. The JavaScript writes the total number of those elements followed by each of their text contents. A conditional test identifies one particular element then applies some formatting to write out the contents of that element and two others containing associated data:

singleElements.html

```
<html> <head> <title>XML Data Island</title>
<script type="text/javascript">
var xmlDoc=new ActiveXObject("Microsoft.XMLDOM");
xmlDoc.async="false";
xmlDoc.load("simple.xml");
if(xmlDoc.documentElement.hasChildNodes)
{
document.write("There are ");
```

```
document.write(xmlDoc.getElementsByTagName("make").length);
document.write(" child elements called 'make'<br/>");
document.write("Their text content is...");
for(var i=0;
    i < xmlDoc.getElementsByTagName("make").length; i++)
  { document.write("<br/>" +
    xmlDoc.getElementsByTagName("make").item(i).text);}
for(var i=0;
    i < xmlDoc.getElementsByTagName("make").length; i++)
{ if(xmlDoc.getElementsByTagName("make").item(i).text
        == "Nikon")
  { document.write("<p>Formatted 'Nikon' matched element
        &amp; siblings:<br/>");
    document.write(
    "<span style='font:bold 16pt;background:silver'>");
    document.write(
    xmlDoc.getElementsByTagName("make").item(i).text);
    document.write(" ");
    document.write(
    xmlDoc.getElementsByTagName("model").item(i).text);
    document.write(" at £");
    document.write(
    xmlDoc.getElementsByTagName("price").item(i).text);
    document.write("</span></p>");}
  }
}
</script>
</head> <body> </body> </html>
```

The lengthy syntax in this script is avoided in the example overleaf which uses variables to shorten the code.

There are 3 child elements called 'make'
Their text content is...
Kodak
Nikon
Fujifilm

Formatted 'Nikon' matched element & siblings:
Nikon Coolpix 880 at £549.00

Done | My Computer

Getting attribute values

The value of any attribute of an element can be addressed using the getAttribute() method of that element. This function takes a single argument that will be the name, in quotes, of the attribute sought. For instance, to address the 'size' attribute of the first occurrence of an element called 'box' would require the code 'Document.getElementsByTagName("box").item(0).getAttribute("size")'.

Alternatively the attribute can be identified by its sequential position in an element that might have several attributes. This is achieved using the item() method of the 'attributes' property of the element. An integer argument is specified with this method to identify the attribute's sequential position in the element tag. For instance, the first attribute will be 'attributes.item(0)', and its 'text' property reveals the value it contains. To get the value of the first attribute of the first occurrence of an element called 'box' uses 'Document.getElementsByTagName("box").item(0).attributes.item(0).text'.

This is logical but does not produce elegant scripts. In order to rectify this, it is a good idea to assign parts of the syntax to variables that can then be used in place of their unwieldy counterparts.

The output below is created when Internet Explorer opens the HTML document on the opposite page. This loads the **simple.xml** document, listed on page 168, then JavaScript builds all the elements' text and attributes' text into a table. The code to actually retrieve the various text items is in individual functions. These are called by each iteration of the loop writing the table rows, and the loop number is passed to each function as the caller's argument:

To see how the readability is improved, compare this example to the previous example on pages 170–171.

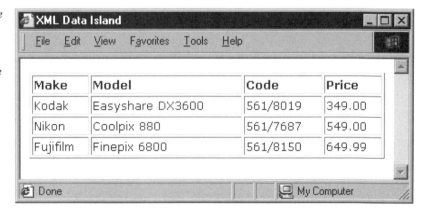

Make	Model	Code	Price
Kodak	Easyshare DX3600	561/8019	349.00
Nikon	Coolpix 880	561/7687	549.00
Fujifilm	Finepix 6800	561/8150	649.99

...cont'd

Use nested single quotes inside outer double quotes to avoid errors.

```
<html> <head> <title>XML Data Island</title>
<script type="text/javascript">

// create a DOM object an load the xml file
var xmlDoc=new ActiveXObject("Microsoft.XMLDOM");
xmlDoc.async="false";
xmlDoc.load("simple.xml");

// check if the root element has any children
if(xmlDoc.documentElement.hasChildNodes)
{
  // declare a variable for each elements' sequence
  var makes=xmlDoc.getElementsByTagName("make");
  var models=xmlDoc.getElementsByTagName("model");
  var prices=xmlDoc.getElementsByTagName("price");

  // functions to get element and attribute values
  function getMake(i){ return makes.item(i).text; }
  function getModel(i){ return models.item(i).text; }
  function getPrice(i){ return prices.item(i).text; }
  function getCode(i){
      return models.item(i).getAttribute("code"); }

  // write a table of element & attribute values
  document.write("<table width='100%' border='1px'>");

  // write column headings
  document.write("<tr><td><b>Make</b></td>");
  document.write("<td><b>Model</b></td>");
  document.write("<td><b>Code</b></td>");
  document.write("<td><b>Price</b></td></tr>");

  // write rows
  for(var i=0; i< makes.length; i++)
  {
    document.write("<tr>");
    document.write("<td>"+getMake(i)+"</td>");
    document.write("<td>"+getModel(i)+"</td>");
    document.write("<td>"+getCode(i)+"</td>");
    document.write("<td>"+getPrice(i)+"</td>");
    document.write("</tr>");
  }
  document.write("</table>");
}
</script> </head> <body> </body> </html>
```

Errors and error handling

It is highly recommended that a specialised XML editor, such as XMLSpy, should be used to create XML documents as they contain integral validation features. These will notify you of any errors before you publish a finished document and so ensure that your code is error-free.

Nonetheless, it remains good practice to include an error handling routine in your scripts to report the cause of any possible errors.

For more on XML editors see page 14, or you can visit XMLSpy on the web at:

www.xmlspy.com

The 'Document.parseError' property is designed especially for this purpose and includes a number of sub-properties describing the nature of an error. The file where the error occurs is identified by the 'Document.parseError.url' property and the line containing the error is pinpointed by 'Document.parseError.line'. The cause of the error is given by 'Document.parseError.reason' and an error code number is contained in 'Document.parseError.errorCode'.

Normally the 'Document.parseError' property is zero unless an error occurs. This fact can be used to make a conditional test at the start of a script to test if the XML document contains any errors.

The XML document below contains an extra </price> tag at the end of the document that causes a deliberate error. When this document is loaded, by the HTML document on the opposite page, the error handling routine reports on the nature of the error and the JavaScript 'else' keyword ensures that the script is halted:

simpleError.xml

```xml
<?xml version="1.0"?>
<cameras>
    <make>Kodak</make>
    <model code="561/8019">Easyshare DX3600</model>
    <price>349.00</price>

    <make>Nikon</make>
    <model code="561/7687">Coolpix 880</model>
    <price>549.00</price>

    <make>Fujifilm</make>
    <model code="561/7663">Finepix 1300</model>
    <price>649.99</price>
</cameras>
</price>
```

reportError.html

```
<html> <head> <script type="text/javascript">

// create a DOM object an load the xml file
var xmlDoc=new ActiveXObject("Microsoft.XMLDOM");
xmlDoc.async="false";
xmlDoc.load("simpleError.xml");

// onerror write an error report
if(xmlDoc.parseError != 0)
{
  var msg="<p><span style='background:red;color:white'>
                          <b>ERROR</b></span>"
  msg+="<br/>Error In File: "+xmlDoc.parseError.url;
  msg+="<br/>Error On Line: "+xmlDoc.parseError.line;
  msg+="<br/>Error Code: "+xmlDoc.parseError.errorCode;
  msg+="<br/>Error Reason: "+xmlDoc.parseError.reason;
  document.write(msg+"</p>");
}

// this code is not executed if a XML load error occurs
else if(xmlDoc.documentElement.hasChildNodes)
{
  document.write("<br/>"
    +xmlDoc.getElementsByTagName("make").item(0).text);
}
</script> </head>
<body>This text will appear even if an error occurs
when loading the XML document!</body> </html>
```

The XML document fails to load because it contains an error – but the HTML page is still displayed.

ERROR
Error In File: file:///C:/MyXML/simpleError.xml
Error On Line: 19
Error Code: -1072896686
Error Reason: End tag was not expected at this location.

This text will appear even if an error occurs when loading the XML document!

Done   My Computer

Cameras application – the schema

The remainder of this chapter builds, step by step, each of the documents needed to create a XML application. XML data will be embedded in a HTML page and extracted by JavaScript.

Turn to page 184 to see how the application will perform.

Firstly, a schema is required to define the element structure for a XML document to contain the data. The XML data will describe features of a number of digital cameras. This builds upon the previous **simple.xml** example on page 168 by adding extra elements to store details about each camera's resolution and the location of a photo image of each camera.

In addition to these two extra elements, a further element will be added to hold each sequence of simple data elements. This more accurately depicts a typical working XML document than the simpler structure of the earlier **simple.xml** example.

The node tree for this structure is shown below:

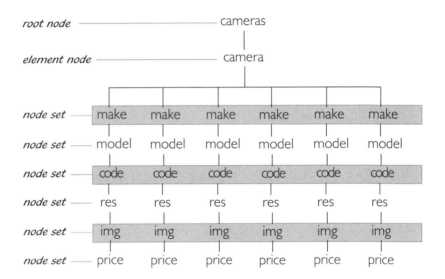

The XMLSchema document on the opposite page creates the above structure with a root element called <cameras> that can contain an unlimited number of <camera> elements. Each <camera> element must contain a sequence of <make>, <model>, <code>, <res>, <img> and <price> elements that hold the actual data about each camera.

cameras.xsd

```xml
<?xml version="1.0" encoding="UTF-8"?>

<xs:schema xmlns:xs="http://www.w3.org/2001/XMLSchema">

<!-- describe the purpose of this schema document -->

<xs:annotation>
<xs:documentation>
This is a schema for a XML document containing data on a
range of digital cameras to include make, model, code
number, resolution, image and price information.
</xs:documentation>
</xs:annotation>

<!-- define an inner element to hold data elements -->

<xs:complexType name="cameraType">
  <xs:sequence>
    <!-- string element for camera make text -->
    <xs:element name="make" type="xs:string"/>
    <!-- string element for camera model text -->
    <xs:element name="model" type="xs:string"/>
    <!-- string element for camera code text -->
    <xs:element name="code" type="xs:string"/>
    <!-- decimal element for camera resolution -->
    <xs:element name="res" type="xs:decimal"/>
    <!-- string element for camera photo url -->
    <xs:element name="img" type="xs:string"/>
    <!-- decimal element for camera price -->
    <xs:element name="price" type="xs:decimal"/>
  </xs:sequence>
</xs:complexType>

<!-- define the root element to hold one, or more, of
                                the above complex type -->
<xs:complexType name="rootType">
  <xs:sequence maxOccurs="unbounded">
    <xs:element name="camera" type="cameraType"/>
  </xs:sequence>
</xs:complexType>

<!-- declare the root element -->

<xs:element name="cameras" type="rootType"/>

</xs:schema>
```

Notice that this schema uses only elements to contain the data. This simplifies the JavaScript code needed to extract the data later – see page 182.

Cameras application – XML data

The XMLSchema document on the previous page defines an element structure that is used in the following XML document to list the data for six digital cameras. This is only a small sample, for demonstration purposes, but the same schema allows for an unlimited number to be added. In practice, XML documents often describe huge sets of data to form a comprehensive database:

cameras.xml

```
<?xml version="1.0" encoding="UTF-8"?>

<cameras
xmlns:xsi="http://www.w3.org/2001/XMLSchema-instance"
xsi:noNamespaceSchemaLocation="cameras.xsd">

  <camera>
    <make>Kodak</make>
    <model>DX3600</model>
    <code>561/8019</code>
    <res>2.2</res>
    <img>kodakDX3600.gif</img>
    <price>349.00</price>
  </camera>

  <camera>
    <make>Canon</make>
    <model>Powershot A20</model>
    <code>561/8112</code>
    <res>2.1</res>
    <img>canonA20.gif</img>
    <price>349.00</price>
  </camera>

  <camera>
    <make>Olympus</make>
    <model>C200</model>
    <code>561/8040</code>
    <res>2.1</res>
    <img>olympusC200.gif</img>
    <price>349.00</price>
  </camera>
```

```
<camera>
    <make>Sony</make>
    <model>DSCP50</model>
    <code>561/8174</code>
    <res>2.1</res>
    <img>sonyDSCP50.gif</img>
    <price>399.00</price>
</camera>

<camera>
    <make>Nikon</make>
    <model>Coolpix 880</model>
    <code>561/7687</code>
    <res>3.34</res>
    <img>nikon880.gif</img>
    <price>549.00</price>
</camera>

<camera>
    <make>Fujifilm</make>
    <model>Finepix 6800</model>
    <code>561/8150</code>
    <res>6.0</res>
    <img>fuji6800.gif</img>
    <price>649.99</price>
</camera>

</cameras>
```

Checking for errors

The XMLSchema document **cameras.xsd** and the XML document shown above, **cameras.xml**, were written in the XMLSpy editor so may be easily checked for errors.

 Clicking the Check Well-formedness button can test each document's XML structure to ensure there are no syntax errors.

 Clicking the Validate button can also validate all documents to ensure that they comply with their respective schema rules.

The listed code for each document is both well-formed and valid so can now be embedded in the HTML document overleaf.

Cameras application – HTML page

This simple HTML document includes the JavaScript file **cameras.js**, that begins on the opposite page. This will embed the **cameras.xml,** from the previous page, and provide functions for the HTML buttons to extract specified XML data.

Most importantly, the HTML code creates a <div> element that is used by the JavaScript functions to output XML data:

cameras.html

Notice that all function calls, except that to 'showPix()', pass an argument to the function that is used to determine what the function returns.

```html
<html>
<head> <title>Digital Cameras</title>
<script type="text/javascript" src="cameras.js">
                                            </script>
</head>
<body>
<form name="f">
<table width="390px" bgcolor="gray" border="0px">
<tr>
<td> <input type="button" value="Prices "
                    onclick="listAll('Price')"> </td>
<td> <input type="button" value="Resolutions    "
                    onclick="listAll('Resolution')"> </td>
<td> <input type="button" value="Cameras Under £500"
                    onclick="range('Under')"> </td>
</tr><tr>
<td><input type="button" value="Codes"
                    onclick="listAll('Code')"> </td>
<td><input type="button" value="Photographs"
                    onclick="showPix()"></td>
<td> <input type="button" value="Cameras Over £500    "
                    onclick="range('Over')"> </td>
</tr>
</table>
</form>

<!-- div to display message and requested data -->
<div id="sho" style="position:absolute;
                    top:80px; width:100%; height:100%;">
Please click one of the buttons to display your choice
</div>
</body>
</html>
```

Cameras application – JavaScript

The following JavaScript code will divert Netscape browsers to a default page or otherwise load the **cameras.xml** data. If no errors are found, the script proceeds to provide functions which can be called with the buttons in the **cameras.html** page shown opposite:

cameras.js

The basic browser check in this example can be extended to be more comprehensive.

```
// check for Netscape version 4.0+ browser
if(!document.all)location="cameras-default.html";

// create a Document object & load a XML document
var xmlDoc=new ActiveXObject("Microsoft.XMLDOM");
xmlDoc.async="false";
xmlDoc.load("cameras.xml");

// onerror write an error report
if(xmlDoc.parseError != 0)
{
 var msg="<p><b>ERROR</b>";
 msg+="<br/>Error In File: "+xmlDoc.parseError.url;
 msg+="<br/>Error On Line: "+xmlDoc.parseError.line;
 msg+="<br/>Error Code: "+xmlDoc.parseError.errorCode;
 msg+="<br/>Error Reason: "+xmlDoc.parseError.reason;
 document.write(msg+"</p>");
}

// if no errors - process the document
else if(xmlDoc.documentElement.hasChildNodes)
{
 // declare a variable for the each elements' sequence
 var makes=xmlDoc.getElementsByTagName("make");
 var models=xmlDoc.getElementsByTagName("model");
 var codes=xmlDoc.getElementsByTagName("code");
 var resolutions=xmlDoc.getElementsByTagName("res");
 var images=xmlDoc.getElementsByTagName("img");
 var prices=xmlDoc.getElementsByTagName("price");

 // internal functions to get element values
 function getMake(i){return makes.item(i).text}
 function getModel(i){return models.item(i).text}
 function getCode(i){return codes.item(i).text}
 function getRes(i){return resolutions.item(i).text}
 function getImg(i){return images.item(i).text}
 function getPrice(i){return prices.item(i).text}
```

Replace unwieldy syntax with variables to keep the code compact.

cameras.js (continued)

Because the loop counter 'i' starts at zero, one is added to count the table cells as '1,2,3,4,5,6', rather than '0,1,2,3,4,5'. So when the count is exactly divisible by 3 the code begins a new table row.

If the range() function is passed an 'Over' argument it will only write XML data when the current price node exceeds 500. Otherwise it will only write XML data when the current price node is below 500.

```
// function to show pictures of all cameras
function showPix()
{
 var list="<table width='390px' border='1px'
                            cellspacing='0px'><tr>";
 for(var i=0; i< makes.length; i++)
 {
  // write make & model in each table cell
  list+="<td>"+getMake(i)+"<br/> "+getModel(i)+"<br/>";

  // write appropriate image in each table cell
  list+="<img src='"+getImg(i)+"'></td>";

  // end table row after every 3 cells
  if((i+1)%3==0)list+="</tr><tr>";
 }
 list+="</tr></table>";

  // output the table
  sho.innerHTML=list;
}

// function to display a specified range
function range(str)
{
 var list="<table width='390px' border='1px'
             cellspacing='0px' cellpadding='5px'>";
 for(var i=0; i< makes.length; i++)
 {
  var condition= (str=="Over") ?
          (getPrice(i) > 500) : (getPrice(i) < 500);
  if(condition)
  {
   list+="<tr><td style='text-align:center'>
                  <img src='"+getImg(i)+"'></td>";
   list+="<td>"+getMake(i)+"<br/> "+getModel(i)+"<br/>";
   list+=getCode(i)+"<br/>"+getRes(i)+"
                              million pixels<br/>";
   list+="<b>£"+getPrice(i)+"</b></td></tr>";
  }
 }
 list+="</table>";
 sho.innerHTML=list;
}
```

...cont'd

*cameras.js
(continued)*

If the loop counter is exactly divisible by 2, that row's background will be silver. Otherwise it will be white.

The argument that is passed to the listAll() function is used to create a suitable table caption and also to determine which XML data to write in the third column of the table.

```javascript
// function to list all data in rows
function listAll(str)
{
  // write appropriate table caption
  var list="<caption>"+str+" List</caption>";

  // write make & model column headers
  list+="<table width='390px' border='1px'
                                  cellspacing='0px'>";
  list+="<tr><th>Make</th><th>Model</th>";

  // write appropriate column header for data
  list+="<th>"+str+"</th></tr>";

  // write rows
  for(var i=0; i< makes.length; i++)
  {
    // toggle row background colour
    list+=(((i+1)%2)==0) ?
          "<tr style='background:silver'>" :
                    "<tr style='background:white'>";

    // write make & model cells
    list+="<td>"+getMake(i)+"</td>
    list+="<td>"+getModel(i)+"</td>";

    // write appropriate third cell on each row
    if(str=="Code")list+=
     "<td style='text-align:center'>"+getCode(i)+"</td>";
    if(str=="Price")list+=
    "<td style='text-align:center'>"+getPrice(i)+"</td>";
    if(str=="Resolution")list+="<td style='text-
        align:center'>"+getRes(i)+" million pixels</td>";
    list+="</tr>";
  }
  list+="</table>";

  // output the table
  sho.innerHTML=list;
}

}
```

Each of the functions in this script is illustrated in action with the illustrations that are shown overleaf.

Cameras application – in action

When the application is first loaded the HTML form displays push buttons and text instruction is displayed below in a *<div>* element.

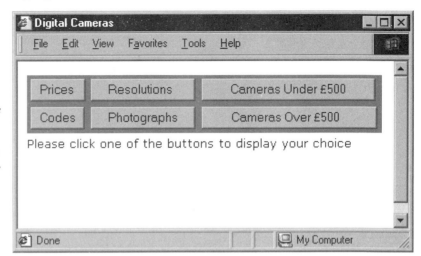

Clicking the 'Photographs' button calls the showPix() JavaScript function that loops through the XML data to create a table. The content of each cell is defined by the contents of the XML *<make>*, *<model>* and *<img>* elements on each iteration of the loop.

...cont'd

Clicking the 'Prices' button calls the JavaScript listAll() function. This creates a table displaying the contents of all the XML <make>, <model> and <price> elements.

The 'Codes' and 'Resolution' buttons display similar tables but the final column shows codes and resolutions respectively, in place of the prices column shown here.

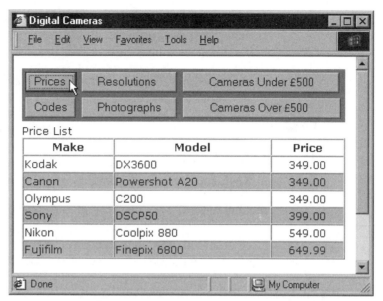

Click 'Cameras Over £500' to call the JavaScript range() function. This loops through the XML data checking the value of each <price> element. When it exceeds 500.00 the function writes a table row using the content of each XML element on that iteration.

The 'Cameras Under £500' button works in a similar way but only creates a table row when the <price> element on the current iteration is below 500.00.

What next with XML?

This book has, hopefully, given you an understanding of the basic XML technologies and has introduced you to some of its many exciting possibilities.

www.w3.org

New aspects of XML are rapidly being developed as more uses are found for the power of XML. These include the XForms specifications that are intended to replace the HTML form controls to become standard across a wide range of user devices.

Other emerging XML technologies focus on security with the XML Encryption and XML Signature languages.

The XML Query working group is adding more features to the XPath language to increase the flexibility of how XML data can be accessed. The declared intention is to make XML databases the defacto standard way to store large quantities of data.

www.adobe.com

One of the most visually exciting uses of XML is for the display of two-dimensional graphics with the Scalable Vector Graphics (SVG) specification. This allows any graphic to be portrayed on a small or large screen without loss of definition. Current versions of the Adobe Illustrator vector graphics program support the SVG format and include an interactivity palette that can add responsive JavaScript code to a graphic. To view SVG graphics Internet Explorer must have the SVG Viewer plug-in installed which is freely available from the Adobe website.

The latest progress of all the above developments, and more, can be found on the W3C website. It is a good idea to regularly visit this site if you are serious about XML development to check the latest recommendations. The site also contains links to many other XML-related sites and is well worth exploring.

msdn.microsoft.com

Implementation of the W3C recommendations is sometimes a matter of interpretation. Practical developments are detailed on the Microsoft Developers Network website where many of the latest XML innovations are announced. Microsoft have adopted XML very keenly and foresee it as a major part of their '.net' strategy with, for example, XML Web Services.

The future for XML looks very bright indeed and we can look forward to seeing many advances with XML technology.

Index

Arranged by technology – find the relevant technology heading then search its entry for the item you require

CSS

DTD

XML DOM

XMLSchema

XPath

XSLT